# Competent Crew

## An Introduction to the Practice and Theory of Sailing

## Companion volumes by the same authors

*Yachtmaster: An Examination Handbook with Exercises*
(Adlard Coles Limited ISBN 0-229-11662-0)

*Yachtmaster Exercises: Navigation Practice Questions and Answers*
(Adlard Coles Limited ISBN 0-229-11715-5)

*Ocean Yachtmaster: Celestial Navigation: An Instructional Handbook with Exercises*
(Adlard Coles Limited ISBN 0-229-11695-7)

*VHF Yachtmaster: A Guide to VHF Procedure*
(Adlard Coles Limited ISBN 0-229-11720-1)

# Competent Crew

## An Introduction to the Practice and Theory of Sailing

Pat Langley-Price and Philip Ouvry

**ADLARD COLES LIMITED**
8 Grafton Street, London W1

Adlard Coles Ltd
William Collins Sons & Co. Ltd
8 Grafton Street, London W1X 3LA

First published in Great Britain by
Adlard Coles Ltd 1985



*British Library Cataloguing in Publication Data*
Langley-Price, Pat
Competent crew.
1. Sailing
I. Title. II. Ouvry, Philip
797.1'24 GV811

ISBN 0-229-11736-8

Typeset by Columns of Reading
Printed and bound in Great Britain by
Mackays of Chatham, Kent

# Contents

# Acknowledgements

We have received much valuable help and advice from organisations and friends too numerous to list in full; however, we would like to express our particular gratitude to the following for permission to use their material:

*Ministry of Defence, Hydrographic Dept.* Compass rose (Fig. 12.3).
*Henry Browne & Son Ltd*, Sestrel porthole compass (Plate 7).

# Introduction

Going out to sea in a small boat is an activity which many people enjoy; yet to those who have not grown up within sight of the sea, the thought of bobbing about all day in unfamiliar surroundings is not necessarily all that attractive. However, when the opportunity occurs and the sun is shining, the companionship enjoyable, the fresh air invigorating, suddenly the whole idea takes on a different meaning. One has a desire to learn more and more about it all.

Now comes the difficult time. It is all so unfamiliar. Every object has a different name. There are lots of ropes and shackles and sails all of which have to be tied together with a variety of knots and bends and hitches. There's coming alongside and casting off, and rowing the dinghy and man overboard drill. . . Man overboard drill? What's this? Accidents? Emergencies? Yes: there are all the safety regulations, collision rules, fire precautions, weather forecasts, and so on. They have to be learned as well. At sea, safety is of paramount importance and everybody who ventures out on the water must be fully aware of the implications of things going wrong. Feeling safe leads to greater confidence. Feeling confident leads to greater enjoyment. And enjoyment is what cruising and sailing is all about.

This book has been prepared as an introduction to seafaring for aspiring sailors who are totally unfamiliar with boats, sailing and navigating at sea. Everything has been explained from first principles. Many diagrams and a glossary at the back are included to help make the nautical language more understandable. At the same time it has been appreciated that, not only will the increasingly competent crew want to know what *he* is expected to do, but he will also want to understand what the skipper and navigator are doing. So without going into detail about the theory of navigating or weather forecasting or the International Regulations for Preventing

Collisions at Sea, this book includes much of the information that a skipper himself would find useful.

The contents of the book are based on the syllabuses of the Royal Yachting Association's practical and shorebased courses for Competent Crew and Day Skipper (as shown in RYA booklet *G15*). Indeed, the only *shorebased* subjects not explained are chartwork and tidal calculations. These are, however, fully covered in the companion book *Yachtmaster: An Examination Handbook with Exercises* (also published by Adlard Coles Limited.) It should be emphasised that there is no substitute for practical experience and that shorebased and practical learning should go hand-in-hand.

The book has been prepared in two parts:

*Part A* is presented as a sequence of events that a new crew member might find on joining a boat going out to sea for the day, either sailing or motoring, and returning that evening to a harbour or to an anchorage. The responsibilities of the skipper and crew are outlined. The skipper is often the navigator, but sometimes the navigator is another member of the crew. Both the skipper and the navigator always appreciate assistance from a willing and competent crew and will normally be only too willing, in return, to explain why things are done the way they are.

*Part B* gives more detail of various aspects of navigation, of weather forecasting, of collision rules, of emergency procedures; and also includes information on first aid, fire precautions, engine maintenance, special manoeuvres and sailing etiquette. The book is completed with a full glossary of nautical terms, and question and answer papers.

Sometimes at sea a boat can be some distance away from other boats and harbours. Sometimes the weather can get worse, the sea get rough and the crew get tired, cold and seasick. Suddenly a pleasant voyage becomes tinged with apprehension. It is now that a skipper really appreciates a competent crew. And what happens if an accident befalls the skipper? Can he be confident that the crew can cope with getting help and sailing the boat home safely? Could *you* be confident that you could get the boat home? This book sets out to give you just that confidence.

We would like to wish all readers very many days of happy and enjoyable sailing and cruising. We are also keen that this book should be complete and unambiguous and would welcome, through the publisher, any correspondence that would enable future editions to be improved.

Pat Langley-Price and Philip Ouvry

# Part A

*Chapter One*

# A New Language

'*Belay the main halyard to the cleat on the starboard side of the mast.*' A typical request heard on a sailing boat, but incomprehensible to a non-sailing person.

To enjoy sailing or cruising in small boats, it is necessary to feel confident; and feeling safe is the best way to inspire confidence. To feel safe it is important to know what everything on a boat is for, and how to use it; and to understand instructions given by the skipper – the person in charge. Yes, the person *in charge*. It is difficult to run a boat by committee, so it is better to have one person whose knowledge and experience is respected by everyone else on board and who has the responsibility of making decisions when required. Every crew member must respect the authority of the skipper, because accidents and emergencies are often caused by lack of discipline on board: not a military discipline but one of understanding and respect.

To achieve this, it is necessary to communicate efficiently. In a maritime environment most objects and actions have special names so it is essential that a new crew member should understand the terminology and should know how to carry out the required actions.

Appendix II gives a glossary of sea terms. You should refer to this every time you come across words or terms which you do not understand.

*Chapter Two*

# About the Boat

## Types of boat

There are motor boats, sailing boats, motor boats with sails, sailing boats with engines, and motor sailers. A motor sailer has a powerful enough engine to complete a passage under power, but a sufficient

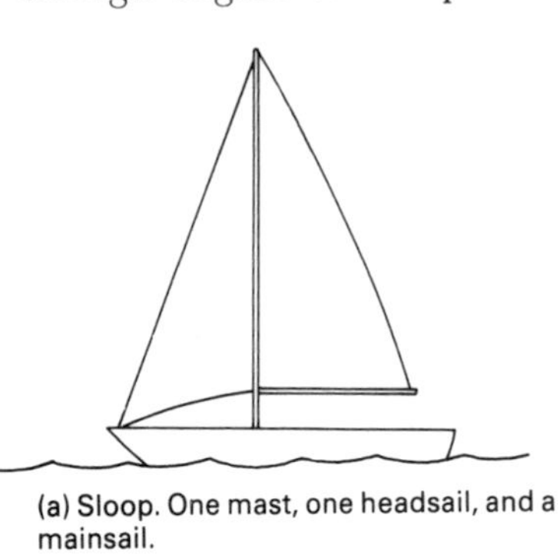

(a) Sloop. One mast, one headsail, and a mainsail.

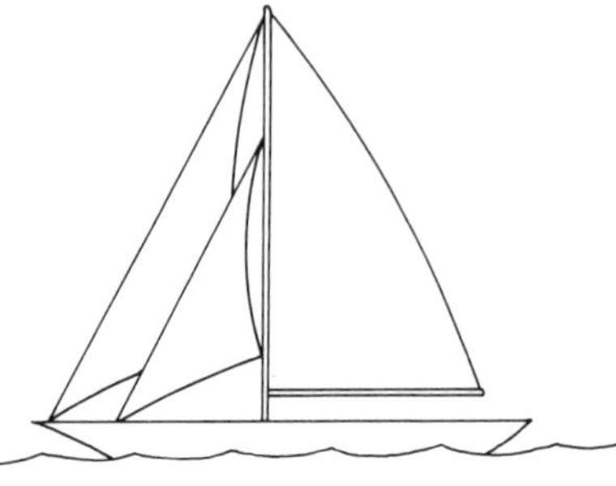

(b) Cutter. One mast, two headsails, and a mainsail.

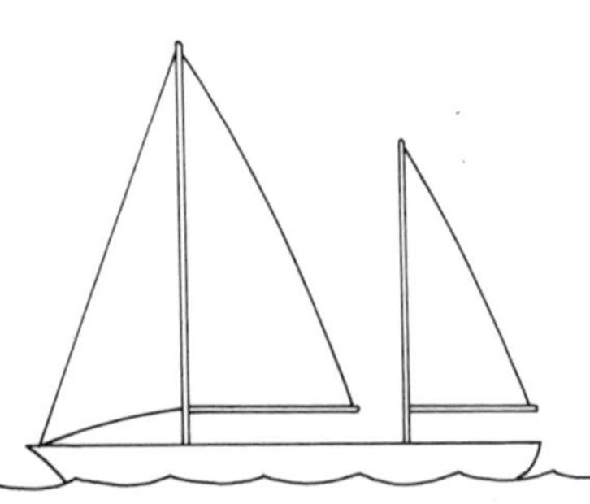

(c) Ketch or yawl. Two masts (main and mizzen). The smaller mizzen mast is aft of the main mast. A ketch has the mizzen mast stepped forward of the steering gear. A yawl has the mizzen mast stepped aft of the steering gear.

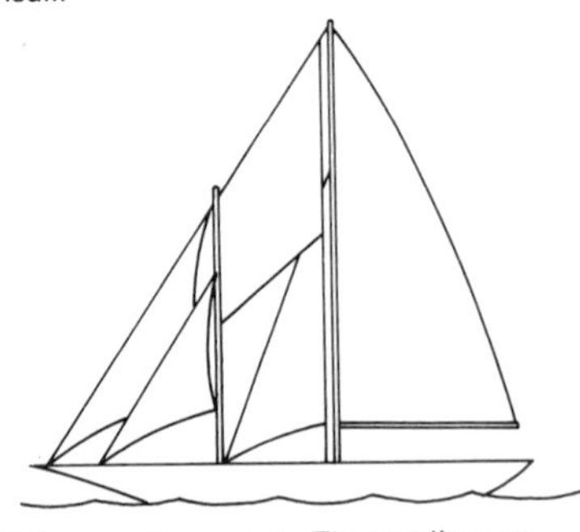

(d) Schooner. Two masts. The smaller one is forward of the main mast.

**Fig. 2.1** Boat rigs.

spread of sail to make good speed with the wind abeam or aft without the use of the engine.

These boats can be rigged in many different ways. Figure 2.1 shows the more common rigs.

However a boat is rigged the same general principles of seamanship apply.

The most common type of rig (the standard rig used in this book) is an auxiliary bermudan sloop (sometimes known as a marconi sloop). This consists of a single masted sailing boat with a triangular mainsail, a headsail and a low-powered auxiliary engine.

Figures 2.2a and 2.2b show parts of the boat; Fig. 2.3 shows parts of the sail and Fig. 2.4 indicates directions relative to the boat.

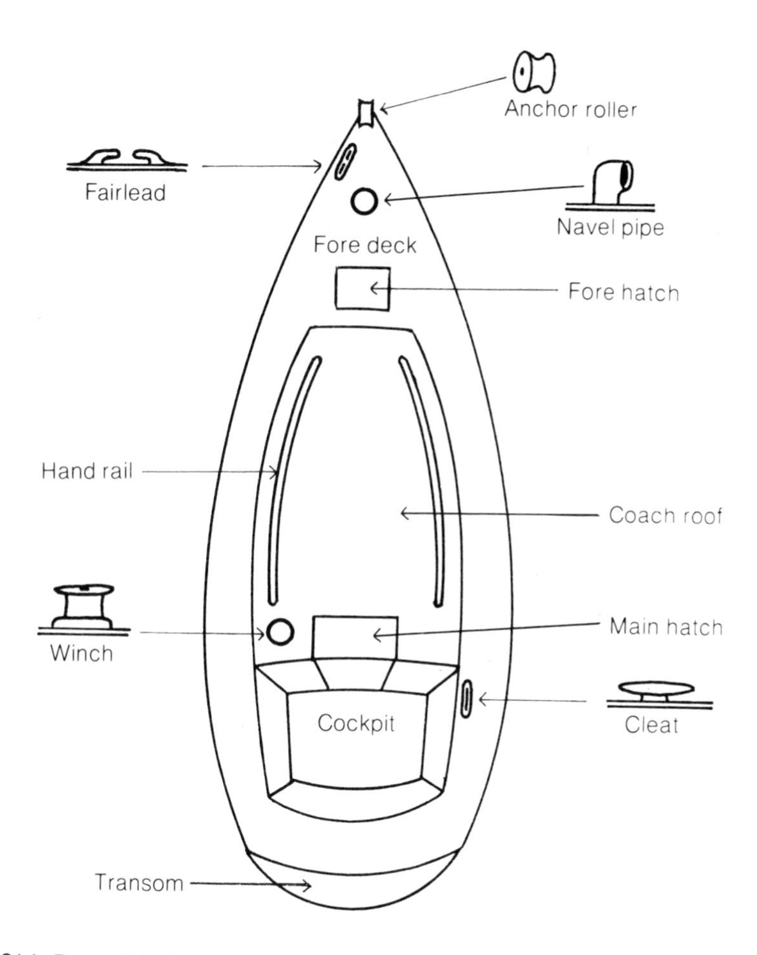


**Fig. 2.2(a)** Parts of the boat.

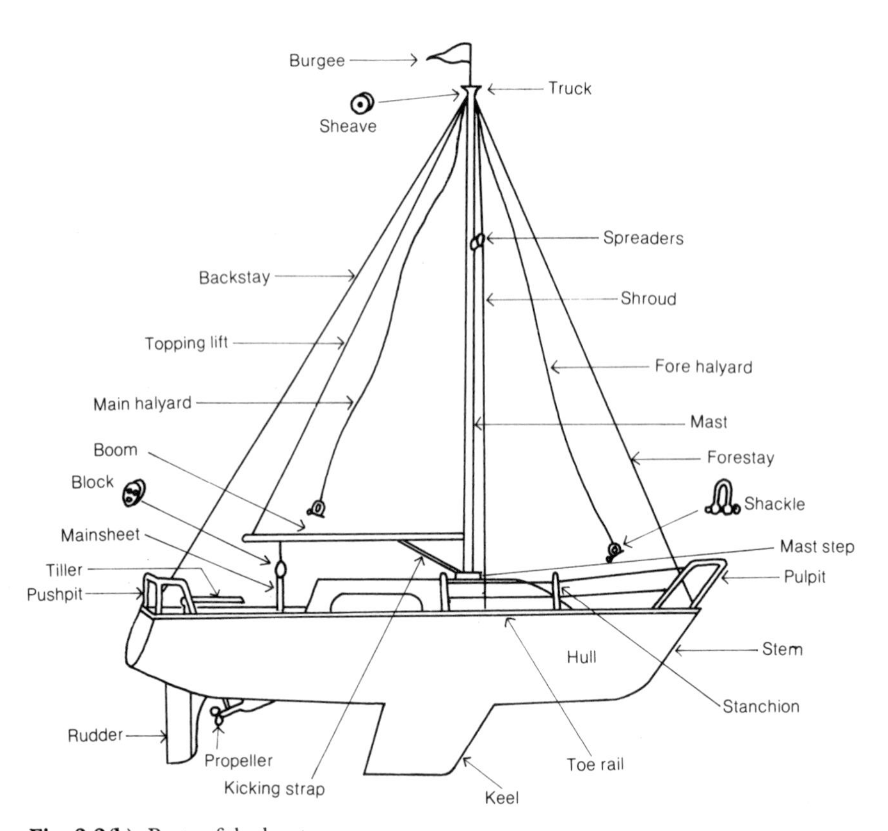


**Fig. 2.2(b)** Parts of the boat.

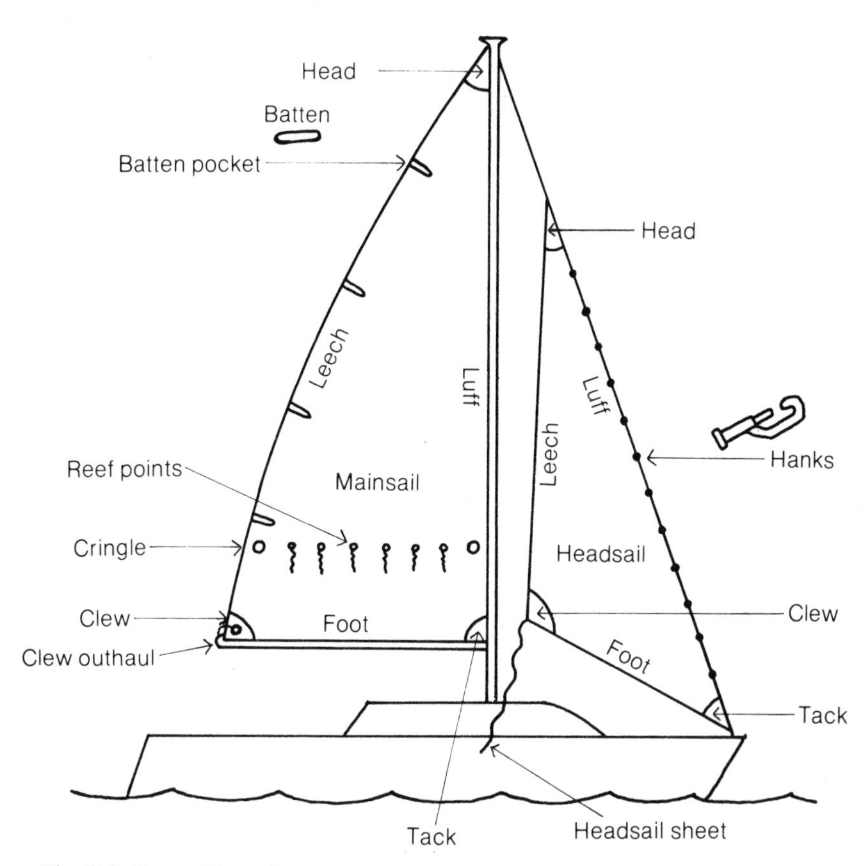


**Fig. 2.3** Parts of the sail.

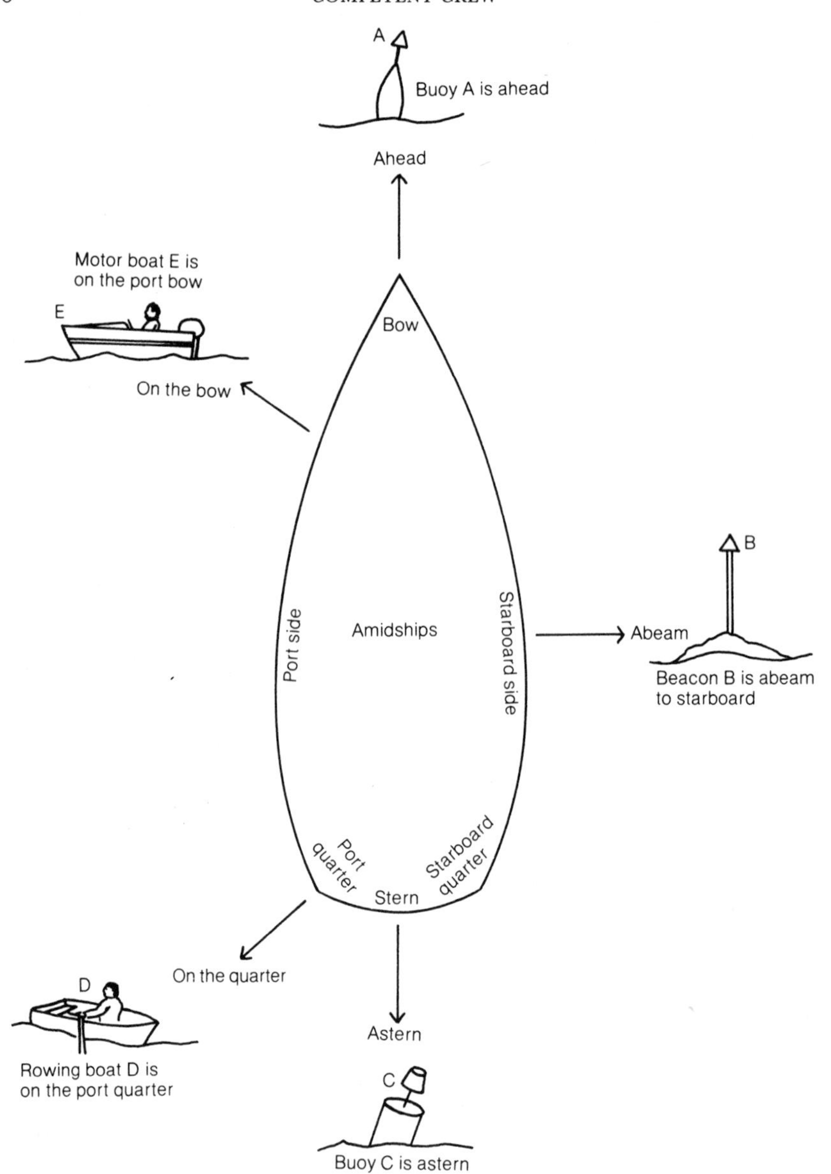


**Fig. 2.4** Directions from the boat.

*Chapter Three*

# Ready to Sail

A boat 10 metres long looks fine at a boat show or in a marina. However, it seems very small when six people with all their gear arrive to go out for a week's holiday. There is not usually enough room for more than sailing clothes and one set of going ashore clothes, and these should be such that they can be stowed bundled up in a soft bag rather than hanging in a wardrobe.

Everything on board must be stowed in its correct place, normally accessible where it will be required. It is important for each member of the crew to know *exactly* where everything is: from coffee/milk/sugar to the bilge pump, and from the hand-bearing compass to the spare torch battery.

## What to wear

The wind at sea is extremely chilling, so always have plenty of warm clothes; usually double the number you may think you need. Once you get cold at sea, it is extremely difficult to warm up again. Remember to include thick socks, gloves and a woolly hat. On top of the warm clothing, wear waterproof and windproof clothing such as oilskins and anoraks. Shoes and boots should be waterproof and have soft non-slip soles, both for safety and to prevent marking the boat's deck.

In hot weather, fewer clothes are required but do not forget suntan lotion, sunglasses (which often prevent a headache caused by glare) and sunhats. Remember the weather can change fast.

## Personal safety equipment

In rough weather and at night time, everyone on deck should wear a safety harness which should be clipped on to a strong part of the boat. Sometimes harnesses are incorporated in oilskin jackets, but generally they are separate and are worn outside. Ideally harnesses should have two clips, so that when moving between different points on the boat the wearer can always be clipped on. Each member of the crew should be allocated his own safety harness which should be adjusted to fit him and ready for immediate use.

In the same way, lifejackets should be allocated to each crew member. These are worn: if there is any likelihood of having to abandon the boat; in thick fog; when going ashore in the dinghy; and by non-swimmers. Lifejackets are brightly coloured yellow or orange so that they can be seen easily in the water, and often have retro-reflective strips on the collars to aid night-time retrieval from the water. Some are fitted with whistles and small water-proof lights for further safety. If buying one for yourself, ensure that its size and buoyancy are adequate for you. A lifejacket should support the wearer on his back when fully clothed, with his head clear of the water. Some lifejackets have to be inflated orally whilst others are self-inflating. For the latter, inflation is achieved: either by squeezing the lever of a carbon dioxide cylinder contained within the lifejacket, or the lifejacket may be designed to inflate automatically on immersion in water.

A buoyancy aid is *NOT* the same thing as a lifejacket and will only assist the wearer to float. Some types can be further inflated orally so that they become a lifejacket.

A sharp knife should also be included in personal safety equipment as it may be necessary to cut a rope quickly in an emergency.

## Preparing the boat for sea

The following is a typical check list for a boat preparing to set sail.

It is the skipper's responsibility to see that these requirements are carried out but the crew must understand what is involved.

1. All gear, both above and below deck, properly stowed so that it cannot roll out of place.
2. Engine checked ready for starting with all cooling water seacocks open.
3. Water tanks full.
4. Fuel tanks full.
5. Spare full gas bottle available.
6. Crew briefed on emergency procedures, including how to launch and board the liferaft.
7. Crew supplied with seasickness tablets as required.
8. All electronic instruments and radios checked for operation.

9. Charts, almanacs and navigational instruments available and up to date.
10. All safety equipment checked and ready for use.
11. Navigation lights, torches and flares checked and ready if any night sailing is intended.
12. Dinghy serviceable, secure and easily accessible.
13. Lifebuoys, danbuoys and safety lines rigged and checked. Crew should be shown the clip-on points to use when wearing a safety harness.
14. Weather forecast obtained.
15. Seacocks on toilets and sinks in seagoing position.
16. All hatches secured.
17. Anchor secure and end of chain or warp made fast inboard.
18. Bilge pumps checked.
19. Fire extinguishers accessible and available.
20. Fire blanket accessible.
21. Battery switch on.
22. Remove sail covers if fitted.
23. Burgee and ensign hoisted.
24. All mooring lines ready for slipping.

*Chapter Four*

# Getting Underway

One of the first jobs you will be required to do is to *bend on* the sails. This is best done before the boat leaves her berth, so that the sails can then be hoisted as soon as she is all clear.

## Bending on the mainsail

Unless the boat has not been used for some time the mainsail will already be fitted to the boom. If it is not, starting with the clew, feed the foot of the sail into the track on the boom and pull it along the boom. When it is all in, secure the tack and tension the foot of the sail by adjusting the clew outhaul (Fig. 4.1). Now fit the battens.

If there are slides along the luff, feed these into the mast track (starting either with the head or the tack of the sail according to the type of mast track fitting) and push the securing pin into the mast after the last one to stop them falling out. If the sail has a rope along the luff (bolt rope) instead of slides, do not feed this into the track until the sail is hoisted. It is usually better not to fit the halyard (by attaching it to the head of the sail) until the sail is about to be hoisted, because without tension on it can get caught up round the spreaders, especially in gusty winds. However, if the halyard is fitted without immediately hoisting the sail, a good way to make sure that enough tension is maintained is to temporarily lead the halyard from the head of the sail down round a mast winch or cleat so that the pull on the halyard then pulls the head of the sail downwards whilst the sail remains stowed. Any foul-ups aloft should then be avoided.

Finally, fold the mainsail neatly over the boom and secure with shock cord (thick elastic) or sail ties (Fig. 4.2)

## Bending on the headsail

Most cruising boats carry several sizes of headsail but the same

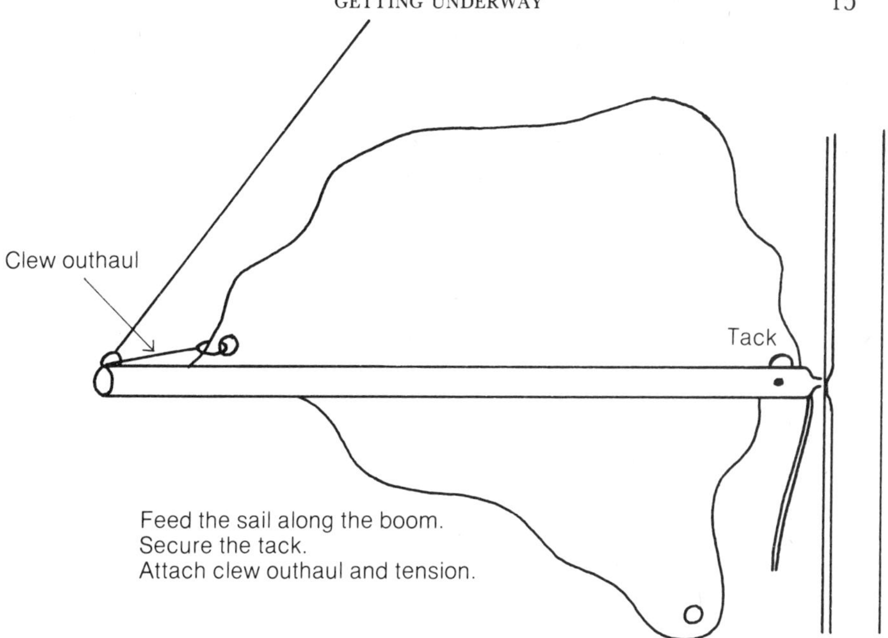


**Fig. 4.1** Bending on the mainsail.

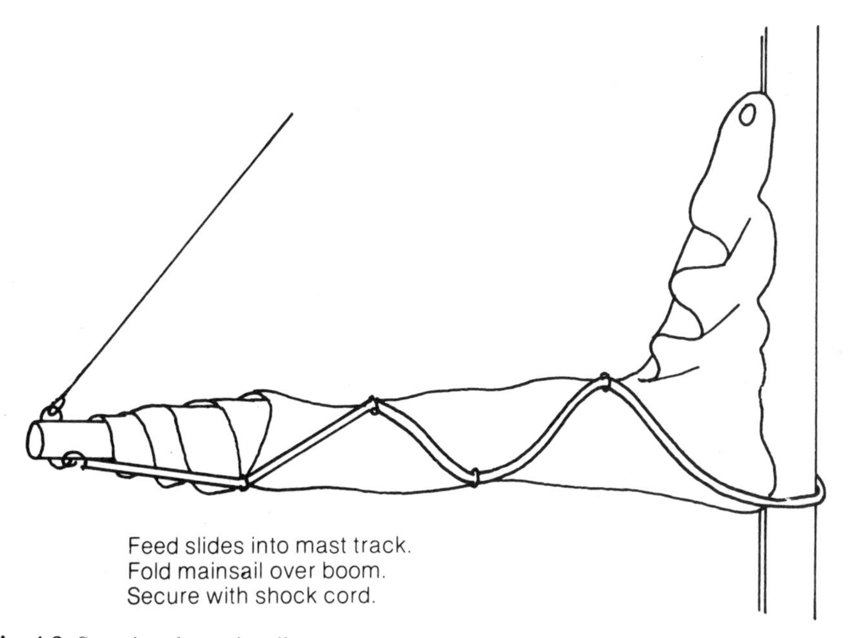


**Fig. 4.2** Securing the mainsail.

principle applies whatever the size. The headsail is secured to the forestay by piston hanks or, in some cases, it fits into a groove on the forestay. It can also be permanently rigged and furled (rolled) around the forestay. This is a modern convenience for easy handling but the basic method described here does not include the self-furling headsail.

Locate the tack, which is normally the corner bearing the sailmaker's name, and shackle it to the appropriate fitting on the stemhead. Next, clip the piston hanks to the forestay making sure that they are all the same way round so that the luff of the sail is not twisted. Now run your hand along the foot of the sail from the tack to the clew to see that it is not twisted, and secure the headsail sheets to the clew using bowline knots (or sometimes a shackle) and lead them through the appropriate blocks to the sheet winches. Tie a stopper knot in the ends of the sheets (see Chapter 10). There is no need to fit the halyard to the head of the sail until it is ready to be hoisted, if it is fitted the head of the sail should be secured to the pulpit so that tension can be kept on the halyard without the sail being pulled up.

Finally, lay the sail along the deck, roll it up and secure to the guardrail with sail ties or shock cord (see Fig. 4.3).

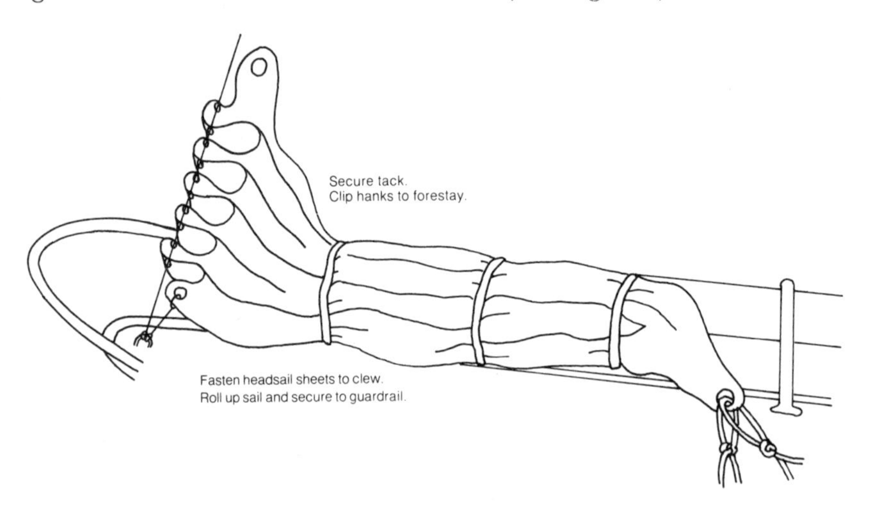


**Fig. 4.3** Bending on and securing the headsail.

## Starting the engine

Nowadays, it is sensible to use the engine to get the boat clear of her berth before hoisting the sails. Most engines are started with an ignition switch and a starter button. However, before starting, the gear lever must be put into neutral and the throttle opened. Ensure that the cooling water seacock is open and, as soon as the engine is running, make sure that the cooling water is circulating (usually by looking at the cooling water outlet). Diesel engines can be used as soon as they are started and do not like to idle too long. Petrol engines perform better when they have warmed up a little.

To stop a petrol engine, turn off the ignition. A diesel engine usually has a separate stop lever which must be reset before the engine is used again.

## Preparing the mooring lines for leaving the berth

If there is neither a tidal stream running nor a strong wind blowing, then leaving a berth in a marina or alongside a quay is straightforward. All lines except breast lines are removed, coiled and stowed. The breast lines are doubled back around a cleat or bollard on the shore so that they can be let go from on board the boat. Thus these lines become slip lines (Fig. 4.4).

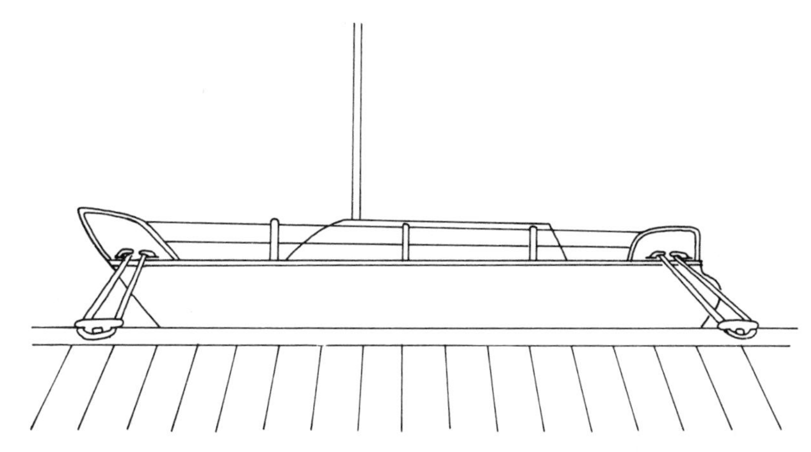

**Fig. 4.4** Rigging slip lines.

If there is a tidal stream running, then one line (usually a spring) should remain attached until the last moment to stop the boat moving forwards or backwards (depending upon the direction of the tidal stream). This spring can also be doubled back as a slip line. The skipper may detail a crew member to standby on deck with a spare fender (called a roving fender) to fend off from any danger.

## Leaving a raft of boats

It is more complicated if your boat is in the middle of a raft of boats moored alongside each other. Often there is no one available to assist on adjacent boats. In this case, making allowance for the tidal stream if there is any, it is necessary to cast off (unfasten) sufficient lines to create a gap through which to depart; then to manoeuvre the boat slowly (by hauling on lines) until it is clear to leave; finally, to make sure that all the other boats are properly secured. It may well be necessary for the skipper to leave a crew member behind to ensure that the other boats are secure, picking him up later from the outside boat of the raft (Fig. 4.5).

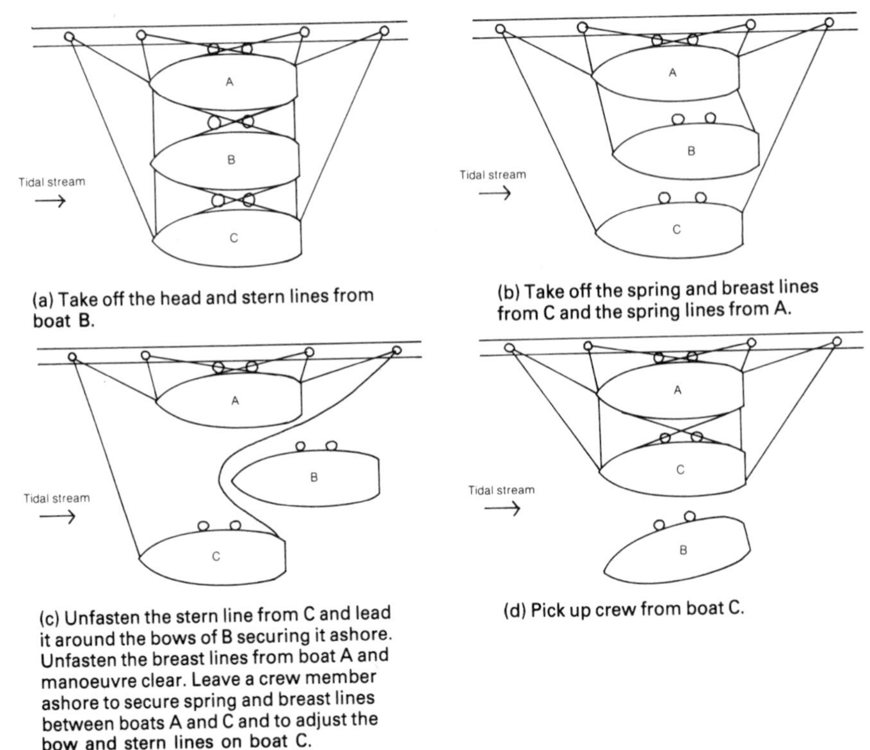


(a) Take off the head and stern lines from boat B.

(b) Take off the spring and breast lines from C and the spring lines from A.

(c) Unfasten the stern line from C and lead it around the bows of B securing it ashore. Unfasten the breast lines from boat A and manoeuvre clear. Leave a crew member ashore to secure spring and breast lines between boats A and C and to adjust the bow and stern lines on boat C.

(d) Pick up crew from boat C.

**Fig. 4.5** Leaving a raft of boats.

In these circumstances it is essential that the crew understands the function of each line and how to secure it without supervision.

## Leaving a buoy

If the boat is moored to a buoy there will only be one bow slip line.

## Stowing lines and fenders

As soon as the boat is clear all lines must be neatly coiled and stowed and all fenders removed and stowed. Any loose ends of rope left around are not only untidy and unseamanlike but can lead to an accident, or trail overboard with the possibility of getting wrapped around the propeller. (See Chapter 10 for coiling.)

## Hoisting the sails

The sails may be hoisted whilst still in the relatively calm waters near the berth. The skipper may require one of the crew to take the helm. Hoisting sails is much easier if the boat is kept moving slowly forward head to wind, with all the sheets kept slack so that the wind does not fill the sails. It is also important that everyone keeps a good lookout for other boats and warns the skipper if any appear to be getting too close.

### THE MAINSAIL

Unshackle the main halyard from its harbour stowage position, check that it is not twisted and shackle it to the head of the mainsail, taking care not to let it go before it is shackled on. The shock cord or sail ties securing the sail can now be released. The boat should be turned head to wind before hoisting the sail so that the wind does not fill the sail whilst it is being hoisted. This will prevent the sail from fouling on the spreaders, but it is a good idea anyway to keep an eye aloft as the sail goes up to check that nothing gets fouled up.

Release the kicking strap and the main sheet so that the boom is free. The halyard is led around the mainsail winch drum and the sail hoisted. (If you are not sure which way the winch drum rotates, spin it by hand first to find out.) It may be necessary to put a couple of extra turns around the winch drum and use the winch handle for the final hoist. Take care not to drop the handle overboard and do not leave it in the winch afterwards. It should be self-evident when the sail is completely up; the luff should feel taut but do not over-strain it.

When the sail is fully hoisted, cleat the halyard, making a coil of the remainder and hang it neatly on the cleat (see Chapter 10). If the halyard is part wire and part rope all the wire must be turned around the winch drum plus two turns of rope before cleating. Remember it may be necessary to lower sails in a hurry so do *not* use locking turns that cannot be quickly undone.

Uncleat the topping lift and ease it off so that the leech of the sail takes the weight of the boom. Tighten the kicking strap, pull in the main sheet just enough to prevent the boom from swinging from side to side as the sail flaps, and cleat it.

THE HEADSAIL

The boat does not need to be pointing into wind whilst this sail is being hoisted. Secure the halyard to the head of the sail. Unfasten the shockcord (or sail ties). Check that the sheets are free to run. Turn the halyard around the headsail winch drum and hoist the sail, using the winch handle if necessary. Cleat the halyard and coil the remainder (as for the mainsail).

When the headsail is hoisted and secured, lead the headsail sheet around the sheet winch drum (initially two turns will be needed) and haul in, using the winch handle if necessary. The sail should be hauled in until it stops flapping. If it is necessary to put an extra turn around the winch this should be done as shown in Plate 1 (Chapter 10). Be careful not to trap your fingers between the sheet and the winch.

WHEN BOTH SAILS ARE HOISTED

The boat can now be set on course, adjusting the sheets of both sails as necessary. It may then be possible to stop the engine. Do not forget to return any winch handles or sail ties to their proper stowage.

## The deck log

As soon as the boat gets underway, the deck log, which is a written record of events, should be entered with the time of departure and relevant details such as: the sails set, engine running hours, wind direction and strength, log reading (from the instrument called a log which records speed and distance), course, barometric pressure and so on. This is all the navigator's responsibility, but every crew member must know how to write up the deck log. In a deck log, times are shown in four figure notation using a 24 hour clock, for example 8.00 am is written 0800. Courses and bearings are given in three figure notation through 360 degrees.

## Lookout

In a small boat the helmsman normally acts as the lookout. However, it is not always easy for him to see around the sails (and other members of the crew) so every person on board must be alert at all times to the presence of any approaching boats. Big ships may look a long way off, but they travel at considerable speeds and distance can quickly be closed.

*Chapter Five*

# Start Sailing

If you have never been on a sailing boat, the mechanics of boat handling seem confusing at first, but a few hours of instruction with an experienced sailor will soon make the essentials clear. If you have sailed a dinghy or sailboard, much of this chapter will be familiar. Keelboats, however, do have their own handling characteristics which must be learnt by sheer practical experience.

## Altering course

The skipper will be constantly giving instructions to ease out or haul in the headsail sheets. Look at Fig. 5.1 and see whether you can find the relationship between the boat's course and the angle of the sails to the wind. You will see that the further the boat's bows are turned away from the wind the more sail is eased out until, when the wind is blowing from behind the boat the sails are fully out.

Figure 5.2 shows various points of sailing. Knowing exactly how much sail to ease out or take in comes with practical experience but a rough guide is to trim the headsail until it stops flapping and then adjust the mainsail to the same angle. When the boat is running before the wind, both sails may be on the same side of the boat or one on either side (which is known as goosewinged) as shown in Fig. 5.2. No sailing boat can sail directly into the wind. Some sail closer to the wind than others. About 45 degrees off the wind is normal on each *tack*, and there will thus be a *no sail sector* of about 90 degrees as shown in Fig. 5.3

To reach a position directly upwind it is therefore necessary to sail a series of zig-zag courses either side of the wind's direction. This process called *beating* to windward is shown in Fig. 5.4. Each course is known as a tack.

Look at Fig. 5.5. Boat A has the wind on the starboard side and the boom is over the port side; she is on *starboard tack*. Boat B has the

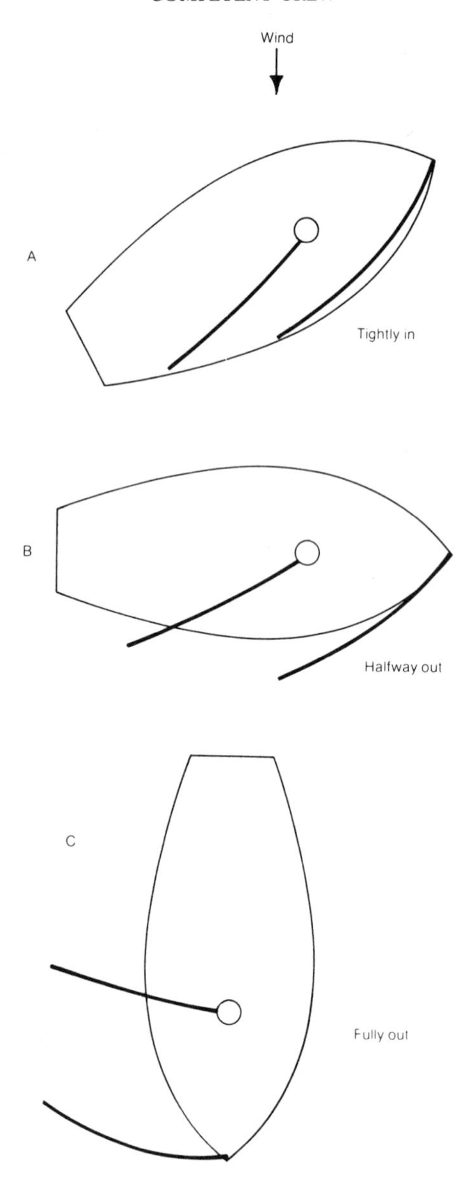


**Fig. 5.1** As the boat turns away from the wind the sails are eased further out.

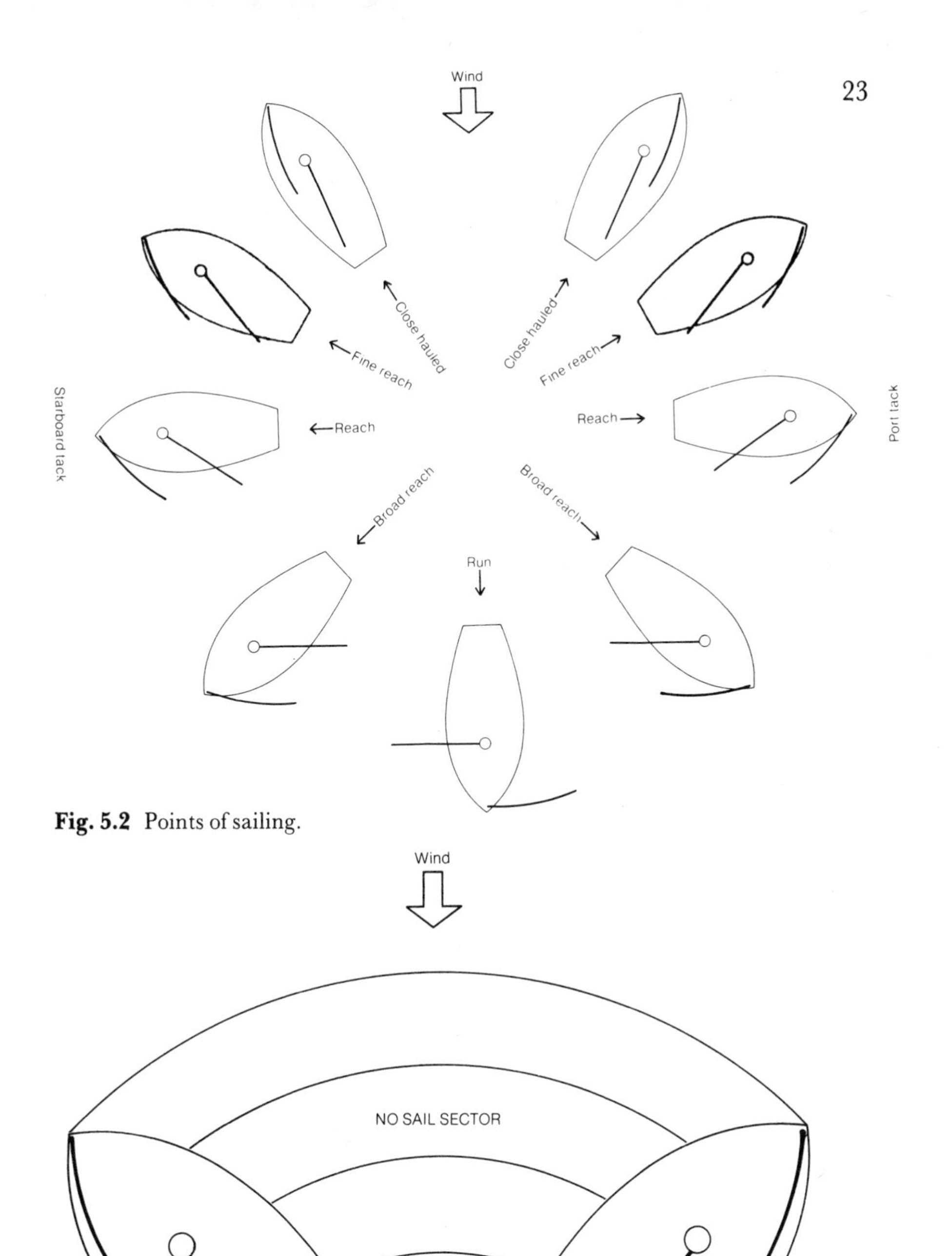


**Fig. 5.2** Points of sailing.



**Fig. 5.3** The boat cannot sail in the NO SAIL SECTOR.

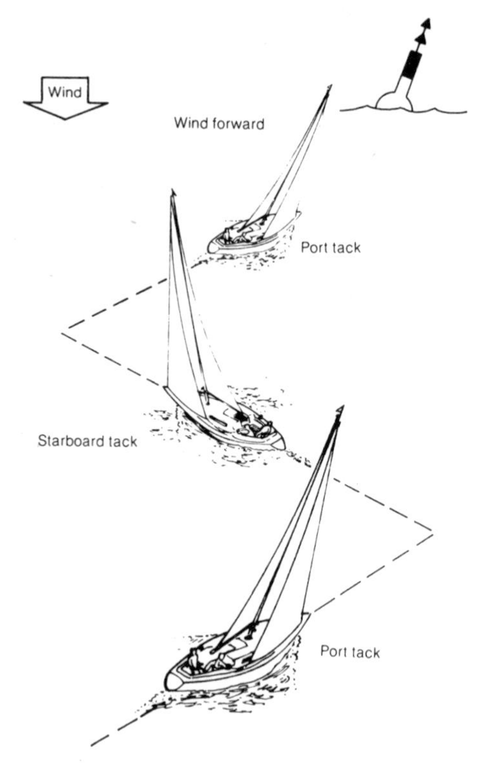


**Fig. 5.4** Beating to windward. To reach the buoy upwind the boat must sail a series of zig-zag courses.

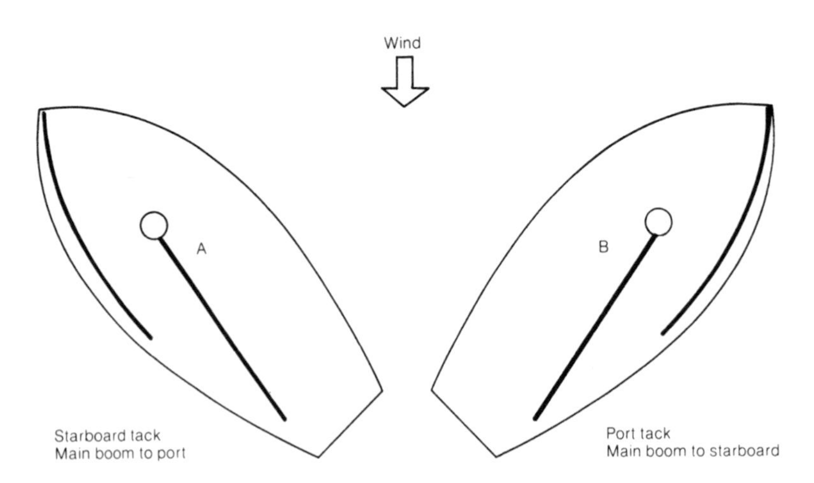


**Fig. 5.5**

wind on the port side and the boom over the starboard side; she is on *port tack*.

## Tacking

The action of altering course from one tack to another when the boat's bows go through the no sail sector is called *going about* or *tacking*.

The boat in Fig. 5.6 is close hauled on starboard tack (bottom). To go about, the helmsman moves the tiller towards the leeward side of the boat. This brings the boat's bows towards the wind. The crew cast off the port headsail sheet and, as the boat's bows move towards

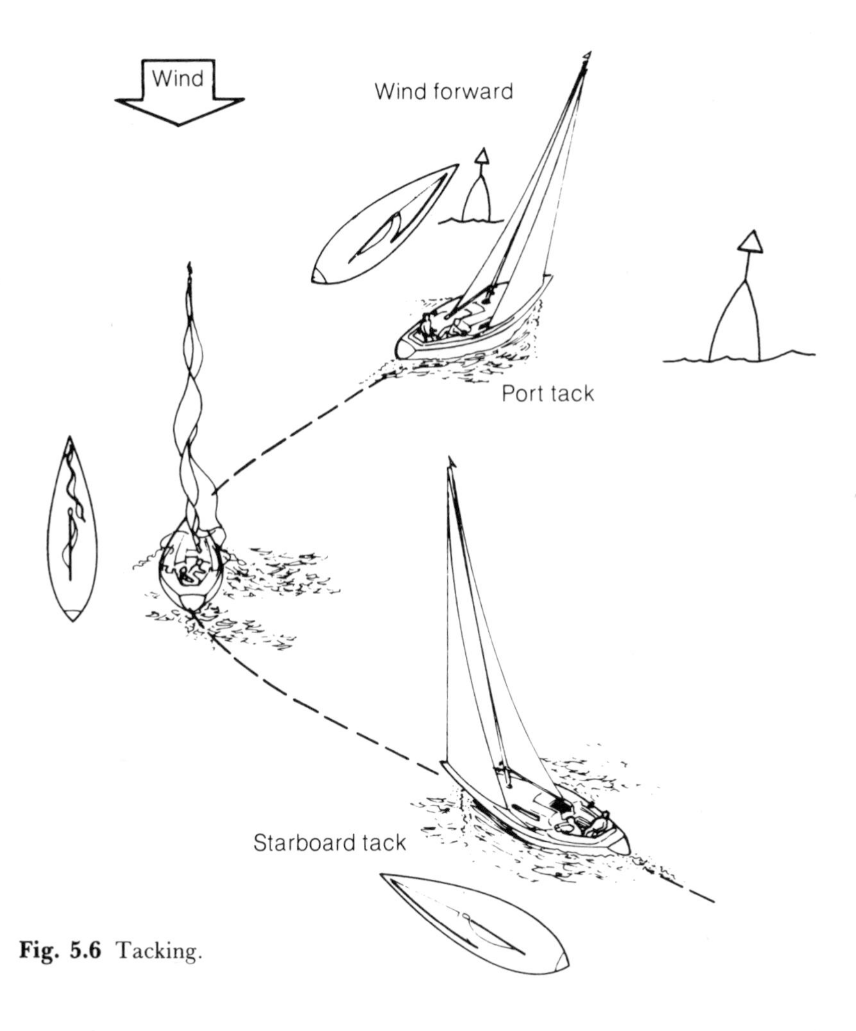


**Fig. 5.6** Tacking.

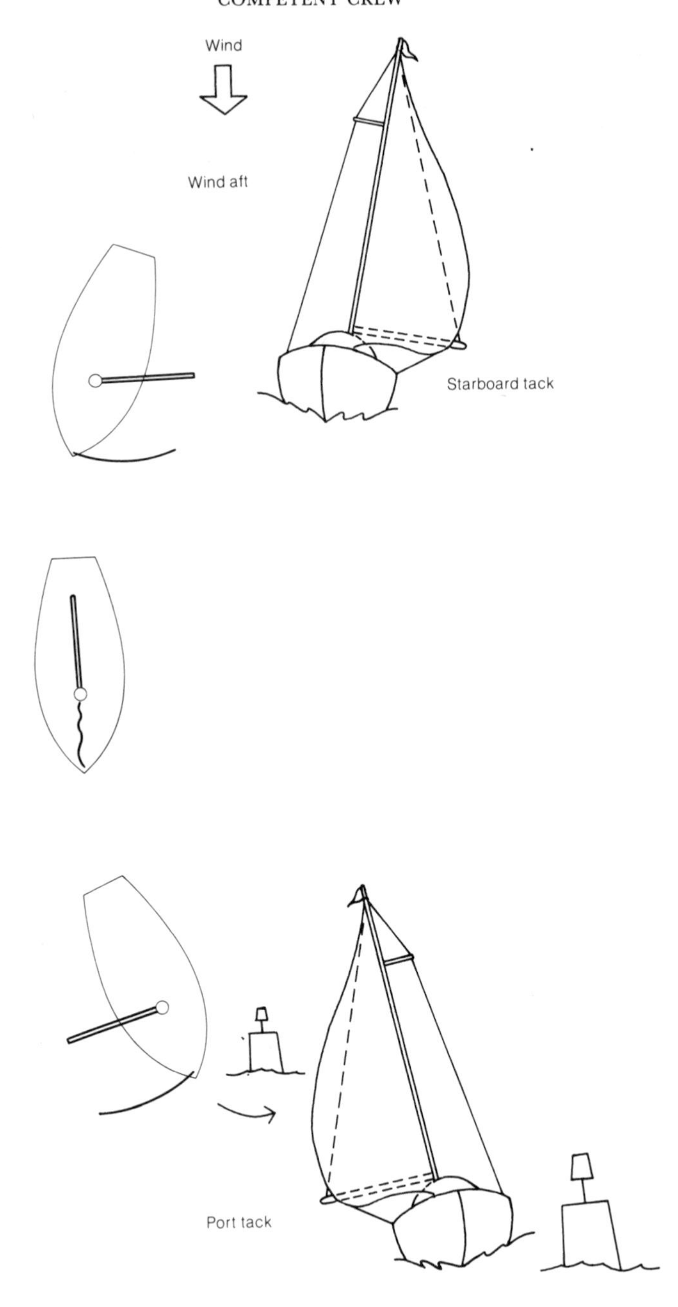


**Fig. 5.7** Gybing.

and through the wind, the sails flap and then fly aross the boat to the other side. The crew now turn the headsail sheet around the starboard winch drum, haul in, and cleat it. If the mainsail needs adjusting this can be done by the helmsman, but when tacking close hauled the mainsheet can normally be left cleated. The boat now sails off on the port tack.

## Gybing

In Fig. 5.7 the boat is initially running on starboard tack with the wind astern. She wishes to pass round the buoy ahead and then alter course to port. She will need to execute a manoeuvre called a *gybe*, in which the stern of the boat passes through the eye of the wind. As the buoy is approached the helmsman centres the *mainsheet traveller*, hauls in the mainsail fully and cleats it. This is to stop the boom flying dangerously from one side of the boat to the other when the sail moves through the wind. He now moves the tiller to starboard which makes the boat's stern travel through the wind. As the boom crosses the boat and the wind fills the sail on the other side, he centres the tiller, and eases out the mainsheet again. At the same time the crew ease out the port headsail sheet and haul in the starboard headsail sheet. (It is best not to let the headsail fly forward of the forestay as it may become twisted around it). The boat is now running on port tack, ready to alter course to round the buoy. The boat's course should remain fairly steady as the boat gybes. An accidental gybe due to careless helming can be extremely dangerous to the crew as well as damaging the boat's rig.

## Steering a course

When close hauled, the course steered by the helmsman is dictated by the direction of the wind. The helmsman endeavours to keep the boat sailing with the sails full (not flapping) and (within limits) he will alter his course to compensate for any small changes in wind direction. The helmsman will regularly assess the mean course that he has managed to steer and inform the navigator accordingly. When reaching or running the helmsman will generally be given a course to steer by the navigator. This may well be a compass course for which he will need to refer to the steering compass. On these points of sailing the sails are trimmed once the helmsman is on course. (Compasses are discussed in Chapter 12.)

All crew members will be expected to take their turn as the helmsman. It is not easy to sail the boat close hauled or steer a steady compass course, but practice is the best way of learning.

*Chapter Six*

# Coming into Harbour

There is much satisfaction in entering a harbour, particularly a strange one, and securing to a berth smartly, efficiently and without unnecessary noise. The procedure for entering harbour must be worked out in advance. If the engine is to be used this must be started and the sails lowered in the approaches to the harbour.

## Approach

For an unfamiliar harbour the navigator will require the crew's assistance in sighting landmarks, taking bearings, watching the depth and identifying leading marks or lights.

Some thought should be given to the possibility of engine failure or the propeller being fouled, and the anchor should be made ready to let go. A fender should also be made ready.

If there is no alongside berth available, it may be necessary to pick up a buoy or moor to piles and so the dinghy should be made ready.

## Lowering the sails

The skipper will decide which sail to lower first; this will depend on many factors, but having the boat under optimum control will be his aim as harbour is approached.

### THE MAINSAIL

The boat should be pointed into the wind to make lowering easier and to keep the sail clear of the spreaders. Uncleat the mainsheet and the kicking strap and tension the topping lift so that it takes the weight of the boom. Uncleat the main halyard and lower the sail. Unfasten the halyard from the head of the sail and secure it in its harbour stowage. Take up any slack and cleat the other end of the halyard. Coil the remainder and hang the coil on the cleat. Haul in and cleat the mainsheet. Tighten the kicking strap. Dependent upon the time available and the weather conditions, the sail can either be folded neatly as shown in Fig. 4.2 or rolled quickly and secured with shock cord or sail ties, to be tidied up later once the berthing or mooring is complete.

### THE HEADSAIL

The headsail can be lowered without the boat being head to wind. However, if it is flying out over the water, it is easier if one of the crew controls the halyard, letting the sail down slowly to prevent it falling into the water, whilst another member of the crew stands up in the bows and gathers it in. When the sail is down, take the halyard off the head of the sail and secure it, then take up the slack and cleat it. Coil the remainder and hang it on the cleat. The sail is then either fastened to the guardrail with shock cord or put into its bag and stowed.

## Preparing for berthing

Mooring lines should be secured to the deck cleats fore and aft and led through the fairleads ready for use (if necessary on both sides). It is a good idea to secure the outboard ends temporarily to the shrouds, which makes them immediately available in the correct position for stepping off the boat, without the possibility of them falling overboard and trailing in the water. The fenders are rigged in their normal place. As the berth is approached two crew members should be ready to step off the boat with the fore and aft mooring lines (Fig. 6.1).

If sufficient crew are available, the skipper will probably detail one member of the crew to stand by with a roving fender, in case the placing of the rigged fenders is not quite right.

## Berthing

### PONTOON BERTH OR ALONGSIDE A QUAY

As soon as the boat is alongside the crew step off with the mooring lines and take a turn around a cleat, bollard or mooring ring to hold the boat until the skipper organises the permanent lines. Do not pull the bow or stern in too hard, but just enough to stop the boat alongside.

**Fig. 6.1** Approaching a pontoon berth.

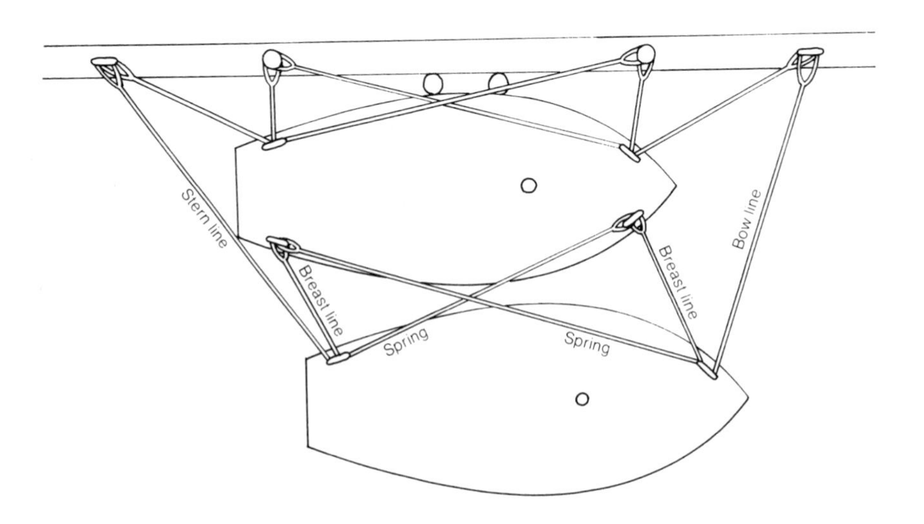


**Fig. 6.2** Berthing alongside another boat.

## QUAYSIDE BERTH WITH SEVERAL BOATS RAFTED TOGETHER

As soon as the boat is alongside the outer boat the crew step off with the bow and stern lines temporarily making them fast to the other boat's cleats fore and aft. It is important to berth the boat in such a way that the spreaders on the two boats will not hit if there is any swell. Head and stern lines will be needed to the shore as well as breast lines and springs to the other boat (Fig. 6.2)

## BERTHED BETWEEN TWO PILES

If there is a boat already berthed between the piles, come alongside her. As soon as the boat is alongside the other boat, the crew step off and temporarily make fast the bow and stern lines to the other boat. Breast lines and springs are rigged to the other boat and the dinghy is used to take head and stern lines to the piles.

If there are no other boats moored to the piles the approach is made into the tidal stream and the bow line secured to the mooring ring on the pile. The boat then drops back to the other pile and secures the stern line (Fig. 6.3). With a cross wind this is difficult and it may be necessary to use the dinghy to row the lines to the piles.

To reduce chafe the line is secured by taking a complete turn around the ring on the pile and then tying a long bowline knot.

## PICKING UP A MOORING BUOY

When securing to a buoy one crew member stands in the bows of the boat with a boat hook, ready to catch on to the buoy and hold it whilst a permanent line is attached. Sometimes the buoy itself can be hauled on board to pull in a larger mooring line which can be secured directly to the mooring cleat.

## AFTERWARDS

When the boat has been securely berthed or moored, all spare lines and sheets are coiled and stowed. The mainsail should be properly folded (if this has not already been done) and the cover put on. If the boat is not to be used for some time the mainsail can be taken off and stowed. The headsail is folded so that it can be put into its bag and stowed (Fig. 6.4).

The boat is cleaned and left shipshape. All seacocks are put into their harbour position. Ensign and burgee are left hoisted or lowered as appropriate (see Chapter 15). The deck log is completed. Stocks of fuel, gas and water are checked and replenished if necessary. A list of defects is made, for attention before the next sail.

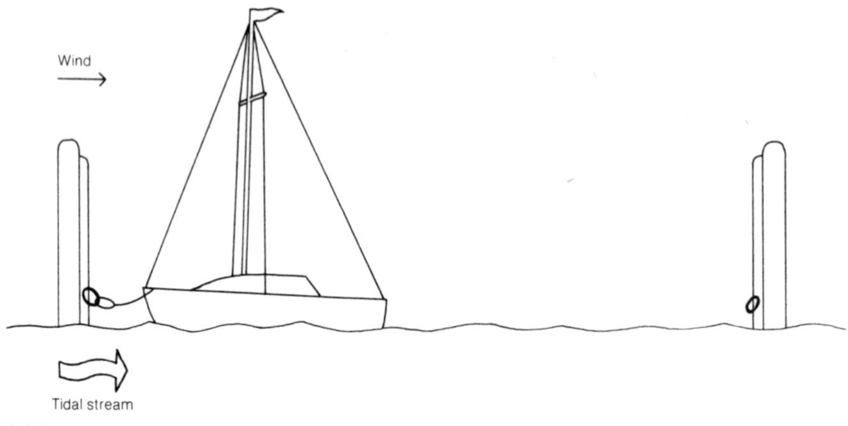


(a) Secure to the upstream pile.

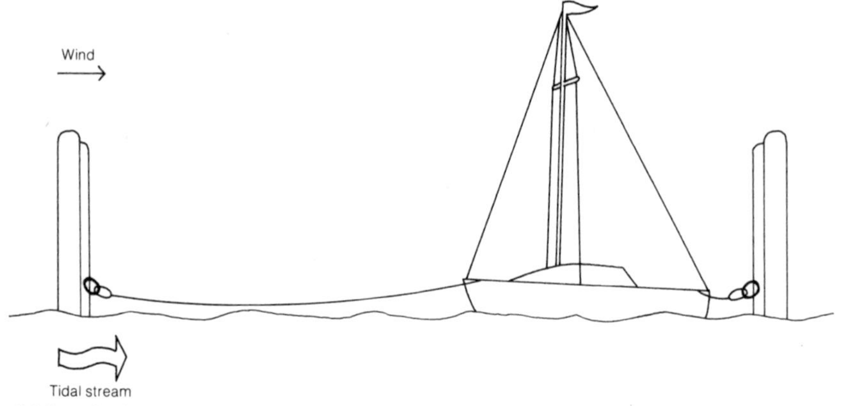


(b) Drop back and secure to the downstream pile.

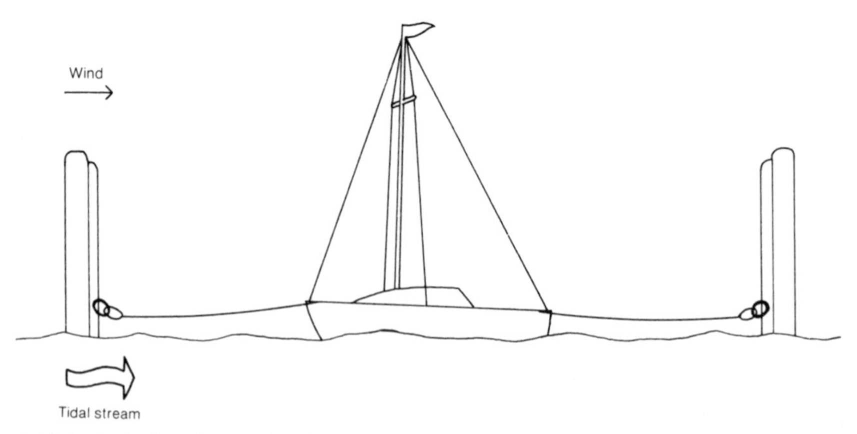


(c) Take in the bow line so that the boat is centred between the piles.

**Fig. 6.3** Securing between piles.

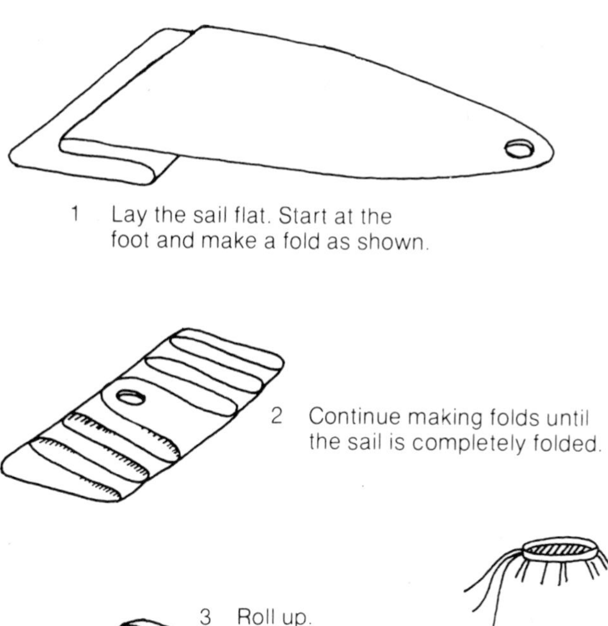


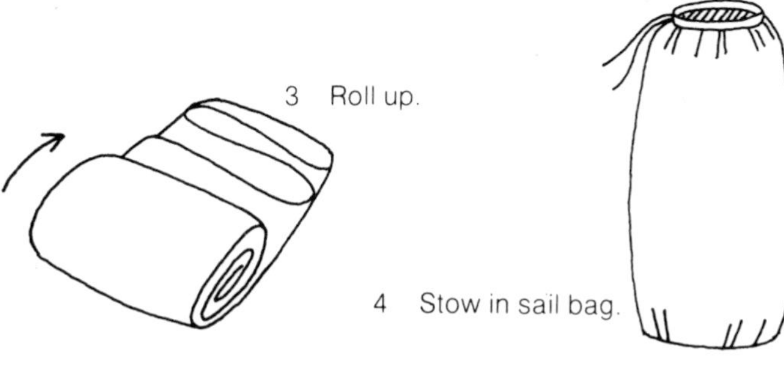


**Fig. 6.4** Folding a headsail.

*Chapter Seven*

# Stopping for a While

## Choosing an anchorage

When your skipper is selecting an anchorage he will be considering the following factors:

1. Good holding ground free from obstructions.
2. Maximum shelter from all expected winds.
3. Clear of obstructions when the boat swings.
4. Sufficient depth of water to avoid going aground.
5. Out of busy areas frequently used by other boats.
6. If it is intended to go ashore, near a suitable landing place.

The ideal anchorage is one where there are no other boats. If it is too crowded, awkward situations can develop should the wind shift. Many approaches to pleasant anchorages are not easy and the navigator will need the crew's assistance to find landmarks, take bearings and check the depth.

## Approaching the anchorage

The approach to an anchorage or a mooring may be made under power or sail. It is important to assess the strength of the tidal stream and its direction in relation to the wind, because this will dictate the line of approach to the anchoring or mooring position. Observation of mooring buoys or lobster pots in the immediate vicinity will help in this; the way the boat will finally lie once anchored or moored can best be gauged by looking at other similar boats already there.

Ideally, if the headsail can be lowered and secured to the guardrail, this should be done to leave the foredeck clear. When the wind and tidal stream are in the same direction the boat will approach on a fine reach, letting the mainsail fly at the last moment. However, if the wind is against the tidal stream and the tidal stream is stronger than or the same as the wind, the boat may have to approach on a run. If the mainsail is left up the boat will not be able to stop, so the helmsman should round up into wind before the anchorage or mooring is reached so that it can be lowered and secured. The approach will then be made using the headsail only. When working on the foredeck with a flapping headsail, the crew must be careful not to get caught up in the headsail sheets especially if using safety harnesses.

## Preparing the anchor

Before reaching the anchorage, the required amount of chain or warp (called cable) can be fed out of the anchor locker and laid out on the deck (called flaking). This ensures that the amount required is immediately ready and that it will not snarl up. Care must be taken to avoid damage to the deck or injury to the crew, particularly if the anchor should go overboard accidentally. If the cable is marked at every 5 metres and it will run freely out of the anchor locker, it need not be flaked.

The amount of anchor cable to be let out (veered) is: three times the maximum expected depth if all chain is used, five times if a combination of warp and chain is used and eight times if bad weather is expected. The pull on the anchor exerted by the cable must be horizontal along the seabed if the anchor is to hold securely (Fig. 7.1). This is why all anchor cables should include at least 6 metres of chain attached to the anchor.

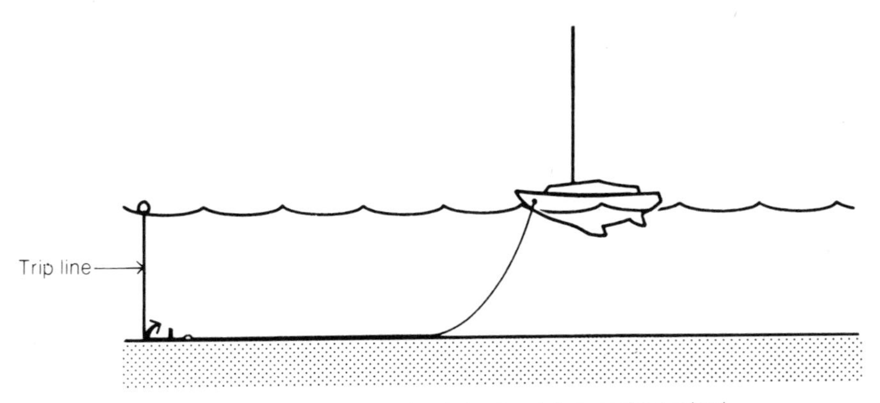


The pull on the anchor is horizontal along the seabed.
A buoyed trip line is rigged to the crown of the anchor.

**Fig. 7.1** Anchoring.

The anchor should be held over the anchor roller ready to let go and not dangled over the bows (particularly if there is any swell).

## Letting go the anchor

The crew should wait until the skipper gives the signal to lower the anchor. This will be when the boat has stopped moving forwards over the ground, which the skipper will judge by selecting suitable shore transits. The skipper will also decide exactly *where* to drop the anchor, in relation to other boats, the depth, the shelter or lack of it from any direction – or even how far it is to row ashore. At this moment the anchor is lifted out clear of the anchor roller and then lowered (letting the cable roll over the anchor roller) until it reaches the sea-bed. As the boat drifts backwards more cable is veered until the predetermined length of cable has been paid out.

The inboard end is secured to a strong cleat or to the samson post so that the rest of the cable will not be pulled out of the anchor locker (Fig. 7.2).

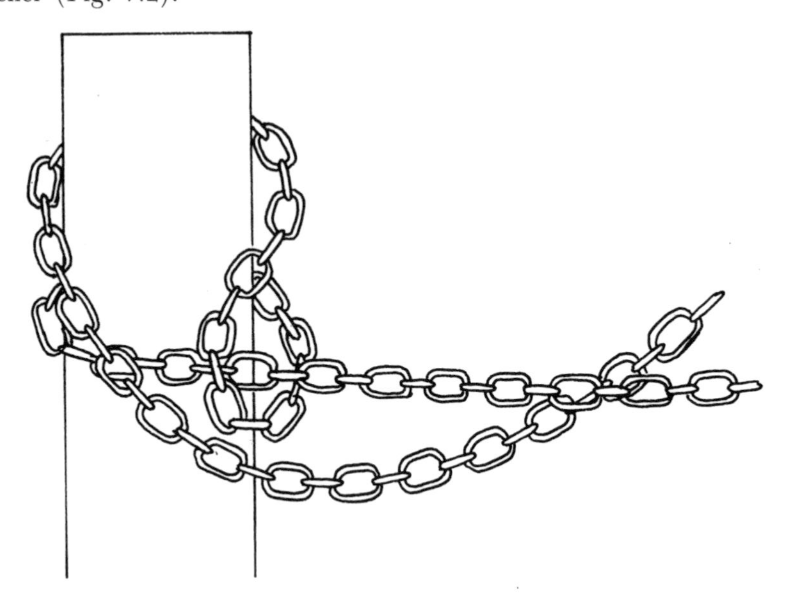

**Fig. 7.2** Securing the anchor cable to a samson post. The cable is turned around the post. A bight of cable is passed under the standing part and then looped back over the top of the post.

The sails, if still hoisted, are lowered, rolled up and secured.

A black ball should be hoisted in the fore part of the boat to indicate to other boats that you are at anchor. At night an all round white light should be shown in the fore part of the boat.

## Anchor bearings

Because anchors do not always take a firm hold immediately, the navigator should select suitable shore transits or use bearings to check whether the anchor is dragging. He may ask the crew to check these frequently for him. He should also periodically check the water depth and watch that the boat does not swing into other boats as the tidal stream changes direction or the wind shifts.

## Leaving the anchorage

Whether this is done under sail or under power will depend upon the number of boats in the anchorage, the weather conditions and the experience of the crew. If the decision is made to sail off the anchorage and the wind and tidal stream are in the same direction, both sails can be hoisted (although it is preferable to hoist the mainsail only so as to keep the foredeck clear). If the wind and tidal stream are opposite to each other and the boat is lying to the tidal stream, only the headsail should be hoisted at first.

When the helmsman is ready, if the wind is light and the tidal stream weak, the crew should take up the slack anchor cable and feed it into the anchor locker until the boat's bows are directly over the anchor. At this point they should tell the helmsman that the anchor cable is *up and down*. If a trip line is attached to a buoy, this should be picked up and any slack line taken in. The anchor should then be *broken out*, that is, extracted from the mud or sand or weed into which it has dug, using the trip line if necessary. The helmsman should be told when the anchor is off the bottom, and when it is clear of the water. The anchor is then brought on board and secured. If conditions permit it should be scrubbed clean before stowing.

When there is a strong wind or a strong tidal stream the boat will either have to be sailed or motored up to the anchor's position, the crew taking in the slack cable as before. In this case the crew must indicate to the helmsman the direction that the cable lies from the boat so that he can manoeuvre the boat to take the tension out of the cable.

## Fouled anchor

It can be most aggravating to find that the anchor has become caught fast upon an obstruction on the seabed. If a trip line has been rigged (Fig. 7.1) the anchor can usually be retrieved by hauling on this. Without a trip line a foul anchor can sometimes be cleared by motoring in the direction opposite to that in which it was laid.

Alternatively the anchor cable can be taken in until it is *up and down*, and a really large shackle or a clump of chain secured to a line dropped down round the taut cable to the anchor on the seabed, where this should slip down over the shank of the anchor towards its crown. The inboard end of the anchor cable is then buoyed and dropped into the water. Now the line attached to the shackle or clump of chain on the seabed is made fast to a stern cleat and the boat motored forward in the opposite direction to that in which the anchor was laid. With luck, the slightly lower point of purchase on the anchor will drag it free of the obstruction.

Occasionally an anchor may become so fouled on the seabed that it has to be left. If this happens, it should be buoyed and its position noted so that it can be retrieved later by a diver.

## Kedge anchor

A kedge anchor can be any lightweight anchor with a short length of chain and a warp. It is used for holding a boat in position if the wind drops and there is a foul tide (for example when racing) or to help pull off a boat that has gone aground. It can also be used in conjunction with the main anchor to prevent yawing in strong winds (Fig. 7.3a)

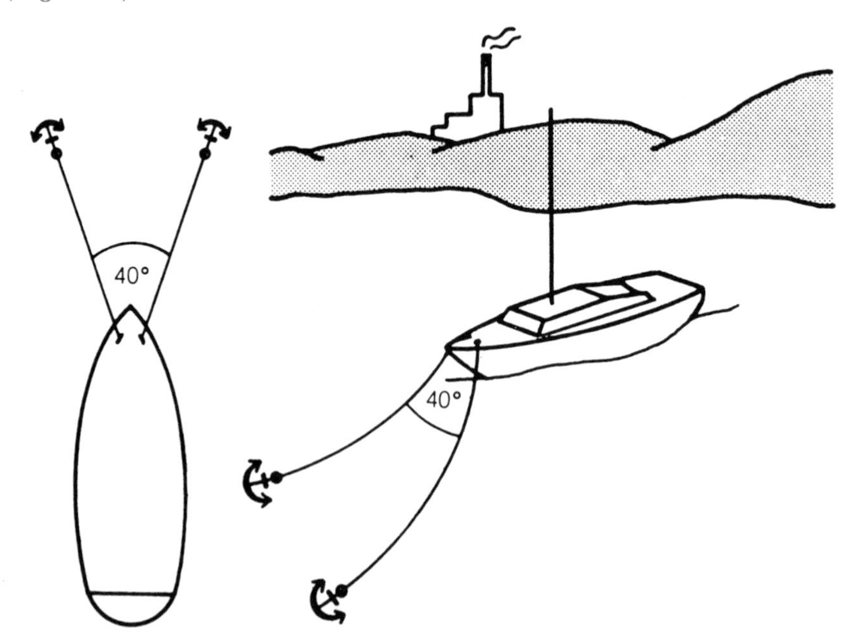


**Fig. 7.3** Mooring with two anchors.

(a) When strong winds are expected, and the boat will therefore be wind-rode and not tide-rode, both anchors can be laid from the bow, with about 40° of spread.

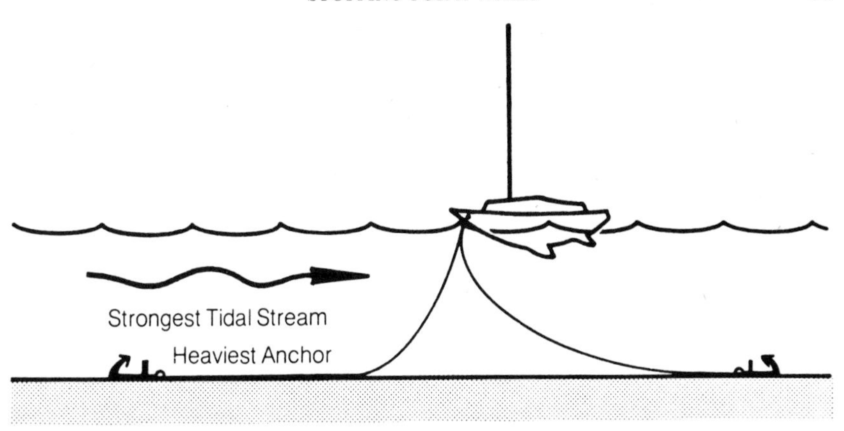


(b) In calm conditions both anchors can be led out over the bow, the heaviest one laid towards the strongest tidal stream; but in a cross wind, both anchors may drag.

**Fig. 7.3** Mooring with two anchors (cont.)

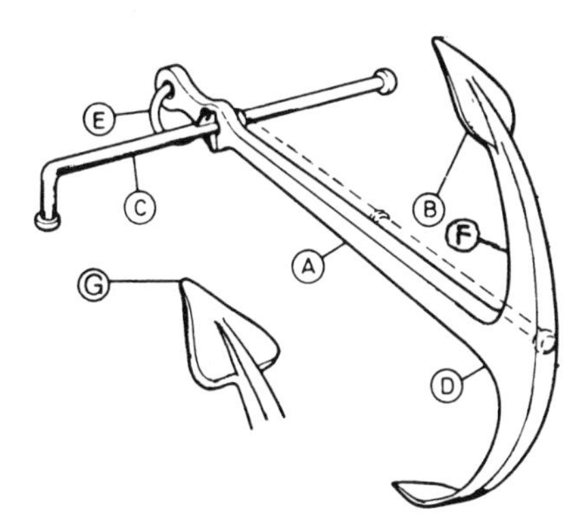


**Fig. 7.4** Fisherman anchor. This anchor has good holding power in sand and mud and it can be stowed flat. The parts of the Fisherman anchor are as follows: A shank, B fluke, C stock, D crown, E ring, F arm, G bill.

Figure 7.3b shows how to lay two anchors to limit the boat's swinging circle. Figure 7.4 shows parts of an anchor. Figure 7.5 shows different types of anchor.

## Mooring

### APPROACHING A MOORING

The procedures are generally the same as for an approach to an anchorage.

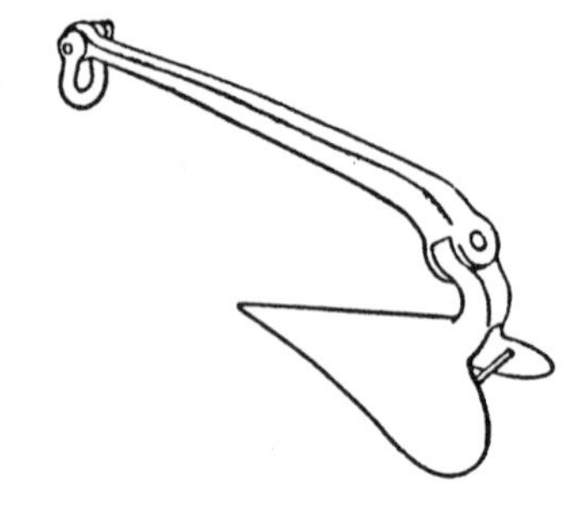

CQR – Holds well in soft sand and mud; not good on hard sand. A lighter anchor required than a Fisherman to give the same holding power.

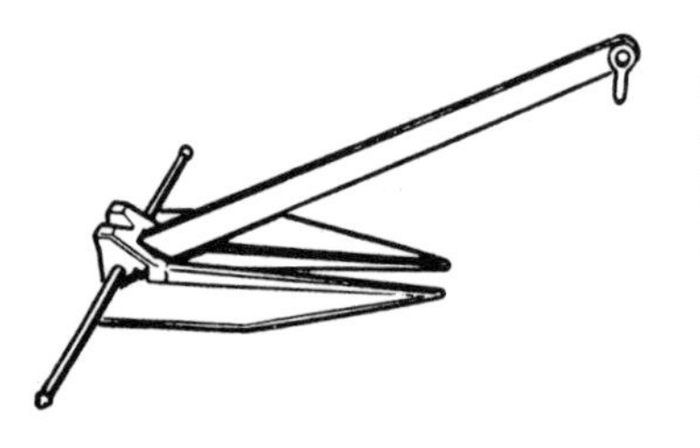

Danforth – Holds well in soft sand and mud; not good on hard sand and seaweed. A lighter anchor required than a Fisherman to give the same holding power. About the same as a CQR. Can be stowed flat.

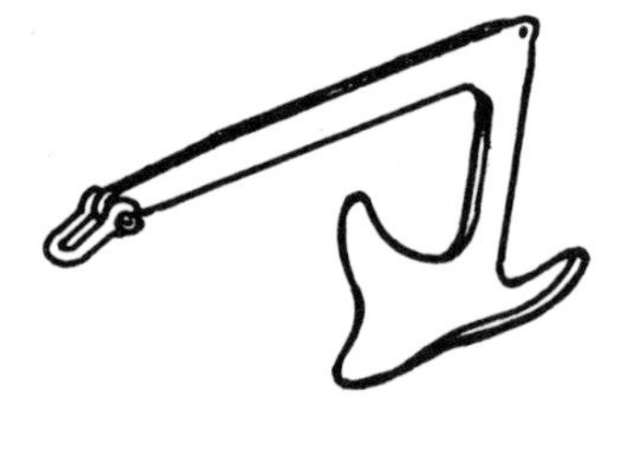

Bruce – A much lighter anchor needed to equal the holding power of the other types.

Rond – A one fluke anchor used for permanent moorings.

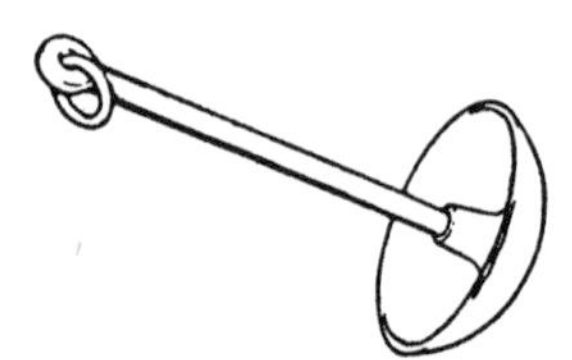

Mushroom – Good holding power. Used for moorings.

**Fig. 7.5** Types of anchor.

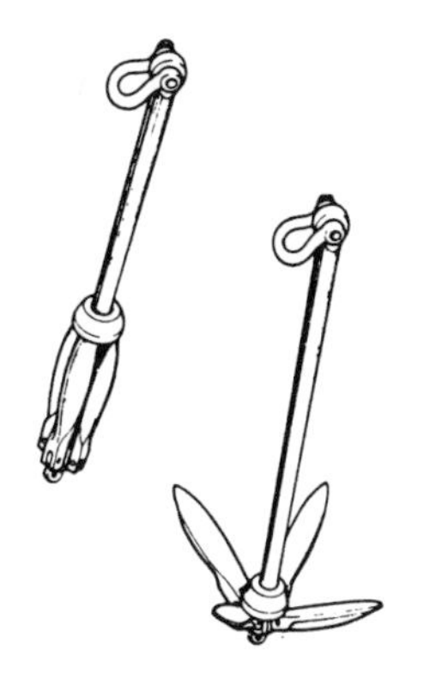

Grapnel – Good anchor to hold on rock. Useful as a kedge.

**Fig. 7.5** Types of anchor (cont.)

PICKING UP A MOORING

One crew member should be ready in the bows with the boat-hook and a line made fast at one end to a cleat on the boat (Fig. 7.6). As the boat's bows stop alongside the buoy, the crew reaches over with the boat-hook and snags the buoy either through the ring on its top or, if there is a pick-up buoy, snags the line under the pick-up buoy. If the buoy is the type with a ring on the top, the crew immediately passes the free end of the line through the ring, brings it back to the boat and secures it to a cleat, after which a decision can be made how to secure more permanently to the buoy. When securing the permanent line, if the ring on the buoy is liable to cause chafe, it is wise to take a complete turn of the line around the ring and then either tie a long bowline or bring the end back to a cleat on the boat. At any points where chafe is likely to occur, such as fairleads or anchor roller, the warp should be protected by a rag or a section of hosepipe. It may be a good idea to rig a second warp in case the original parts.

If the buoy has alongside it a small pick-up buoy which is attached to a mooring chain or a heavy line, it should be picked up and taken on board. There is usually a line joining the small buoy to an eye in a chain or heavy warp, which should then be taken on board and secured around a cleat or the samson post.

LEAVING A MOORING

If the wind and tidal stream are in the same direction both sails or

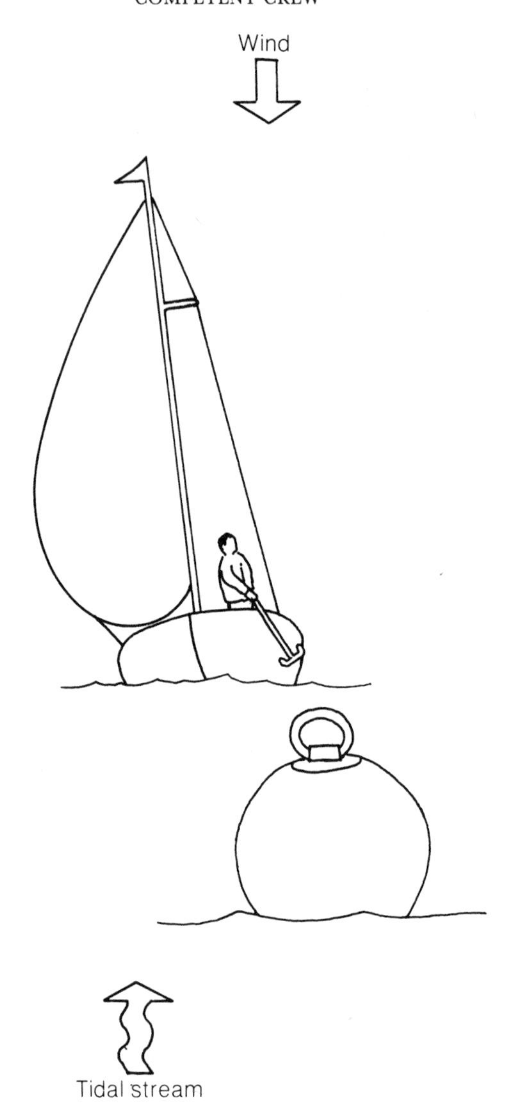


**Fig. 7.6** Picking up a mooring.

just the mainsail can be hoisted. If the wind is against the tidal stream the headsail only will be used initially with the boat rounding up into wind to hoist the mainsail when clear. The crew should rig a slip line or uncleat the chain and hold it on one turn around the cleat ready to let go. If the headsail is hoisted this can be *backed* to ensure that the boat's bows pay off in the desired direction.

In crowded moorings the skipper may decide to do these manoeuvres under power.

## Launching the dinghy

To get ashore from an anchorage or mooring, the dinghy will be required. Most small boat dinghies are inflatables. It is the crew's job to inflate and launch the dinghy and fit the outboard motor if one is to be used. Make sure that the dinghy painter is secured to the boat before launching and fasten a line to the outboard motor before lowering it into the dinghy. When the outboard motor has been clamped on to the dinghy, use a line to secure it to the dinghy so that if it jumps off its brackets it will not be lost overboard. Be careful of fuel spillage.

Normally the dinghy will be boarded by going down a ladder alongside or at the stern of the boat. Step into the middle of the dinghy and always board a dinghy gently: sudden movements of weight cause capsizes. Wear a lifejacket. If going ashore at night a torch must be carried ready to use if any other boats are around.

Inflatable dinghies are difficult to row in a stiff breeze. If you are not used to rowing, get some practice when the opportunity presents itself, but start upwind of the destination. They are also quite difficult to handle under outboard power, so again practice is necessary. Do not forget to take the oars in case the engine stops.

The dinghy can either be carried ashore, or moored at the landing place. If it is moored it may be necessary to leave a long painter to allow for the fall of the tide. The oars, if left aboard, should be well secured.

Having returned to the boat, the dinghy can be deflated and stowed if it is not needed again. Alternatively it can be taken on board and lashed down for the night, or secured alongside as shown in Fig. 7.7. It is not a good idea to tow a dinghy behind a boat except in calm weather, because it can easily turn over or fill up with water.

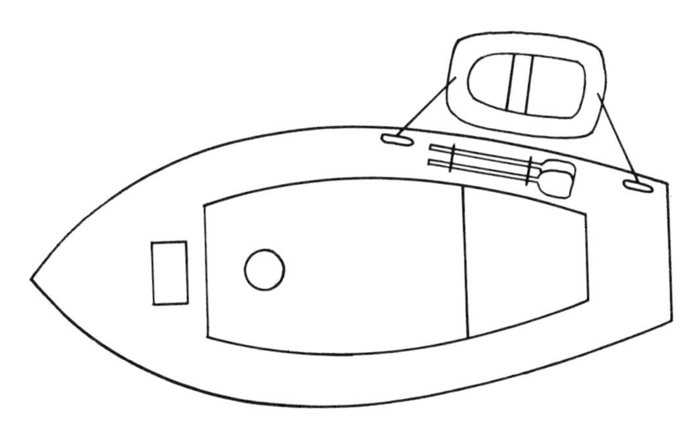

**Fig. 7.7** Securing the dinghy alongside.

## Emergency use of the dinghy

If the boat's engine fails, the dinghy with outboard engine can be secured alongside as shown in Fig. 7.8 to give the boat some steerage way. This is more effective than towing a heavy keelboat with a light dinghy.

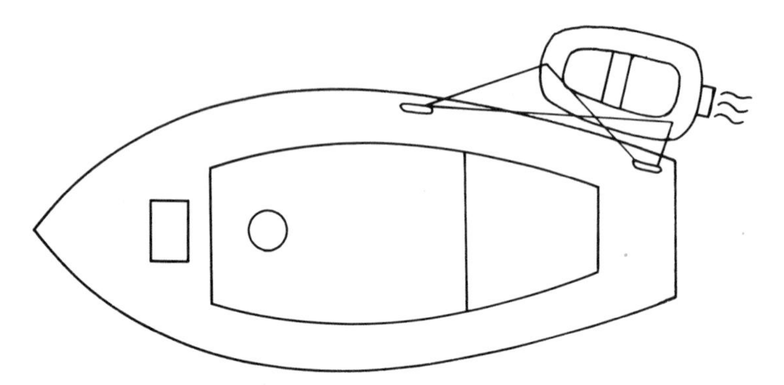

**Fig. 7.8** Emergency propulsion. For emergency propulsion springs are needed as well as bow and stern lines.

*Chapter Eight*

# Bad Weather

The skipper will listen regularly to weather reports and forecasts and so he will usually have some warning of bad weather approaching.

## Fog

At the approach of a fog bank or in decreasing visibility the navigator's immediate action will be to try to fix the boat's position by using any available landmarks. He will have been keeping a record of fixes in the deck log and so should know at all times the approximate position.

In dense fog there are two major dangers:

1. Being run down by a larger boat.
2. Going aground.

The crew will be expected to keep as quiet as possible, to keep a good look out, and to listen for fog signals and other boats' engines. It may be necessary to position a crew member in the bows of the boat, well away from the noise of the boat's own engine, to do this effectively.

All crew must be wearing lifejackets.

The radar reflector should be hoisted and use made of any electronic instruments such as the echo sounder and the radio direction finder (RDF).

The correct fog signal must be sounded (see page 106).

In order to minimise navigational error as much as possible, maintain a steady course and speed. If there is little wind the engine may have to be used, in which case it is a good idea to stop the engine periodically to listen out for any approaching boats or fog signals. The skipper will need to decide whether to stay out in deep water or go inshore and anchor.

## Gales

If gales are expected the skipper will set a small headsail, possibly a *storm jib*, and reduce the area of the mainsail by *reefing*.

The crew should see that all gear above deck is securely lashed down and all gear below deck properly stowed and lashed down if necessary. All hatches should be checked to see that they are secure and the washboards put in position. The cook of the day should prepare sandwiches and hot drinks in vacuum flasks in case it is not practical to do so later.

Seasickness tablets may be needed.

### REEFING

Often a decision to reef is made too late or the sail area reduced insufficiently. The boat may appear to be sailing well downwind, but she could be greatly over canvassed if she had to turn into wind in an emergency. Figure 8.1 shows three methods of reefing the mainsail.

Reefing at sea is made easier by *heaving-to* (Fig. 8.2). When hove-to, a boat will be steady with little forward movement; she will, however, drift sideways, so plenty of sea-room downwind is required. If it becomes necessary to reef, all crew members on deck must be wearing a safety harness and be clipped on.

## Lee shore

In strong winds it is extremely dangerous to sail close to a shore on to which the wind is blowing, called a *lee shore*. The boat can easily be blown on to it and badly damaged. If the route to the intended destination involves taking such a risk it is safer to alter the route and even the destination. Heavy seas can quickly build up in shallow waters so it is sometimes necessary for the skipper to decide to stay out at sea in rough weather rather than risk entering a harbour with an unsheltered approach (such as a lee shore). It is a very difficult decision to make, particularly if the crew are cold and seasick and night is approaching. It is at this time that the skipper needs the full support of his crew, so it is important that the crew realise fully the risks involved.

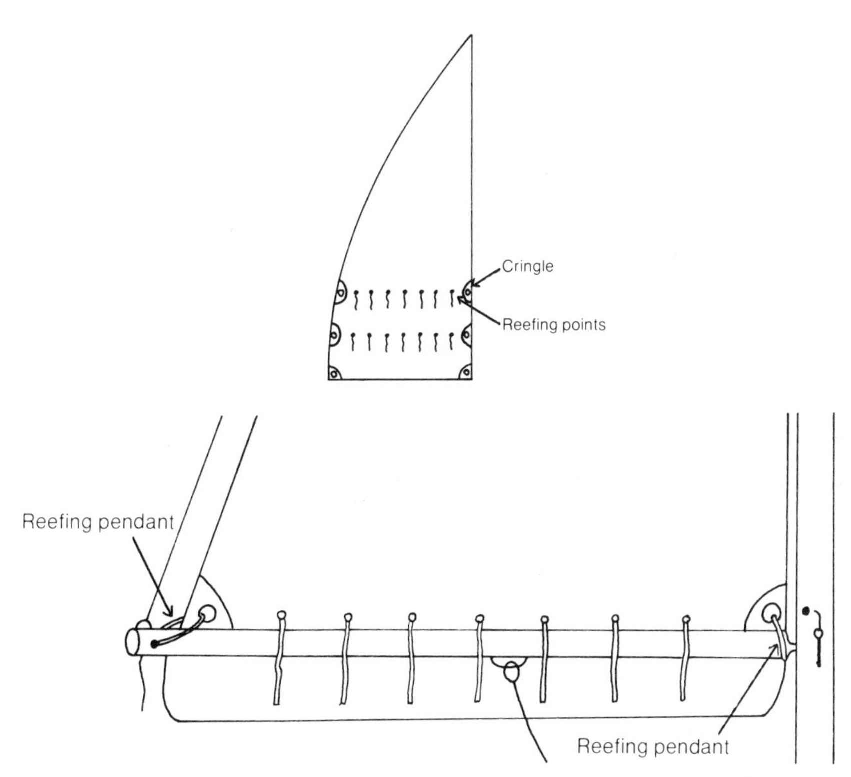


(1) Reefing points. (a) Ease the kicking strap and tension the topping lift. Take the securing pin out of the mast so that the luff of the sail can be pulled out of the mast track. Uncleat the main halyard and lower the mainsail to a position where the luff cringle can be lashed to the boom.
(b) Feed a short length of line (called a reefing pendant) through the luff cringle and lash it to the boom. The pendant for the leech cringle may be permanently attached to one side of the boom and all that is necessary is to pass it through the cringle and secure it to a block on the other side of the boom.

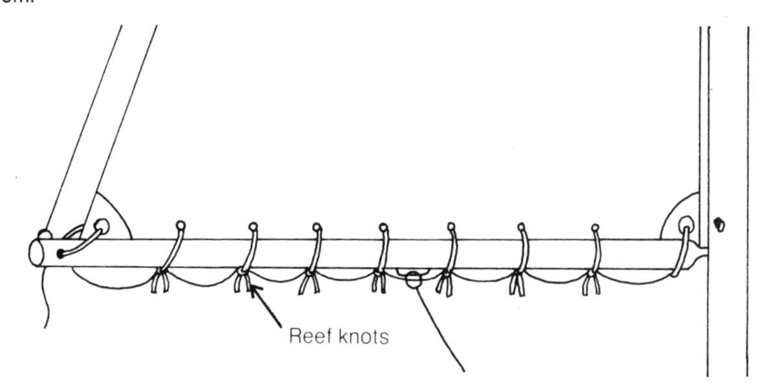


(c) Hoist the sail, replace the securing pin in the mast, cleat the halyard, ease out the topping lift and tension the kicking strap. (d) Roll up the loose sail and secure by tying together (under the boom) the reefing points from either side of the sail. Use reef knots for this. (e) When taking the reef out, untie the reefing points before the reefing pendants or the sail may tear.

**Fig. 8.1** Reefing

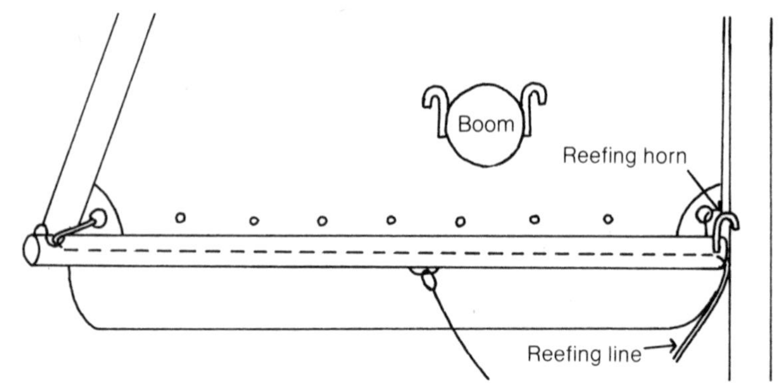


(2) Slab reefing. (a) Ease the kicking strap and tension the topping lift. Take the securing pin out of the mast so that the luff of the sail can be pulled out of the mast track. Uncleat the main halyard and lower the mainsail to a position where the luff cringle can be hooked over the reefing horn.
(b) Hook the luff cringle over the reefing horn and pull the leech cringle down to the boom by using the reefing line. (This is attached to the boom near the end, fed through the leech cringle and then back through the boom, via a block.)

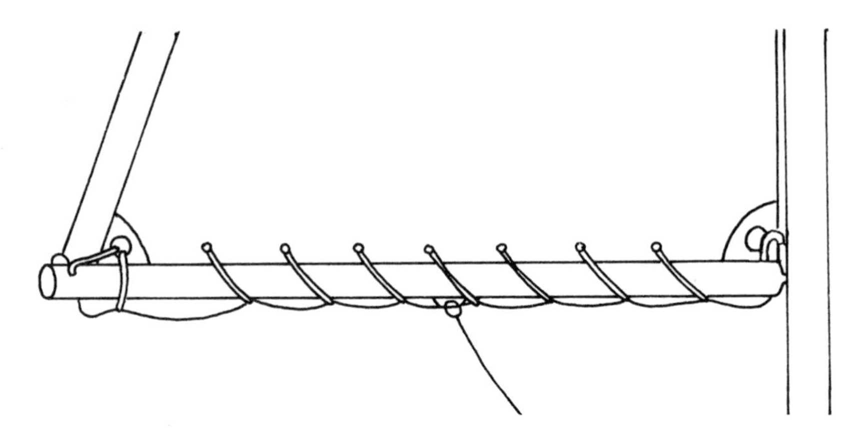

(c) Hoist the sail, replace the securing pin, cleat the halyard, ease out the topping lift and tension the kicking strap. (d) Roll up the loose sail and spiral a light line through the eyelets in the sail and around the boom, securing it at both ends. (e) When taking the reef out, remove the light line first.

**Fig. 8.1** Reefing (cont.)

(3) Roller reefing.
(a) Take off the kicking strap and tension the topping lift. Take the securing pin out of the mast so that the luff of the sail can be pulled out of the mast track. (b) Uncleat the halyard and ease down the sail, turning the reefing handle at the same time. The sail should be pulled tight at the leech to make it roll evenly. Care should be taken to prevent the luff fouling the reefing gear. (c) When the sail has been reduced sufficiently, remove or secure the reefing handle, hoist the sail, replace the securing pin, cleat the halyard and ease out the topping lift. With this method any amount of sail can be reduced, but the sail does not set as well as when using the other methods. The kicking strap cannot be used because the sail is rolled around the boom. One solution is to fit a reefing claw over the rolled sail.

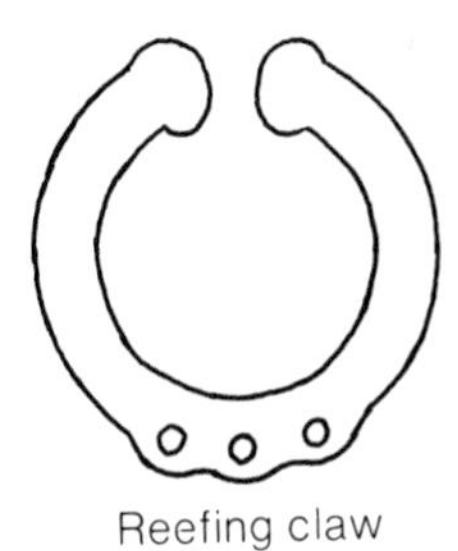

Reefing claw

For all methods any battens which interfere with reefing should be removed.

**Fig. 8.1** Reefing (cont.)

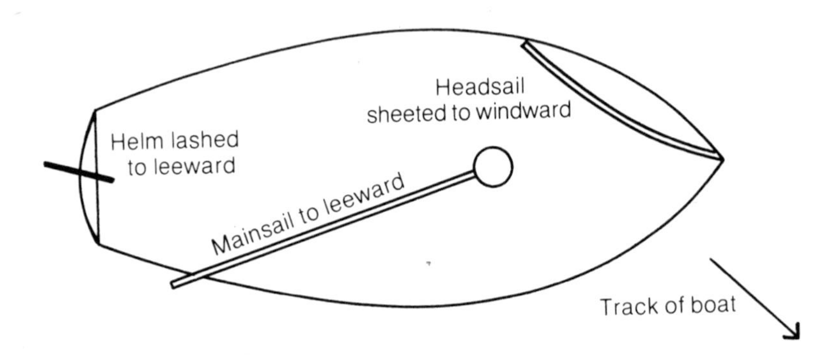


**Fig. 8.2** Heaving-to. The helm is lashed to leeward and the headsail sheeted to windward. The drive of the mainsail is thus counteracted.

*Chapter Nine*

# Special Manoeuvres

## Grounding

Going aground on a muddy bottom in fair weather on a rising tide is no emergency. Usually, going astern under power and rocking the boat will get the boat off again. But going aground on a falling tide can be embarrassing. It is necessary to act quickly to avoid being stuck for several hours. A tow from another boat (if available) is ideal, provided she does not go aground as well. Launching the dinghy to lay out a kedge anchor can be done rapidly by an efficient crew. The crew then haul on the anchor cable to try to pull the boat clear.

With a fin keeled boat it is sometimes possible to spin the boat around on the keel and use the full power of the engine to get back into deep water.

If the boat is stuck for the duration of the tide, then it is sensible to try to ensure that she falls uphill or away from the wind and flood stream. It may be necessary to use an inflatable dinghy as a large fender. A kedge anchor should be laid out into the tidal stream (or wind) ready for pulling off as soon as the boat refloats.

## Towing

### RECEIVING A TOW

Good communication with the towing vessel is essential. The boat which is to be towed should provide the tow line. This should be made fast around the mast, the samson post or a strong cleat, and led out through the foremost fairlead or the anchor-roller. (A rag or cloth can be used to reduce chafe.) As the towing vessel approaches, the tow line should be passed across, if necessary by throwing a lighter *heaving line* joined on to the heavier tow line. If the tow is expected to take a long time or the weather is rough, then the tow line will have to be long and should be weighted to prevent *snatching* (that is, the tow line snapping taut). To weight the line either a length of chain can be used or a heavy weight (such as the anchor) secured to the tow line about half a boat's length ahead of the towed boat. The towed boat should lower its sails and aim to steer directly behind the towing boat.

### GIVING A TOW

It is quite likely that the boat in trouble is undermanned or the crew are tired. She may be drifting on to a lee shore. It is possible that your skipper may want to transfer a crew member to the boat in trouble so that he knows that there is somebody on board who understands what is required. It is often sensible for the towing boat not to lose steerage way, so be prepared to jump across to the other boat as the skipper steers slowly past (remember to wear a lifejacket). Once on board you can help the boat in trouble to get ready to receive a tow.

On the towing vessel, once the tow line has been received on board, a turn is taken round a strong cleat aft. The tow line should be *surged* (eased out slightly) as the strain comes on so that there is not a sudden jerk on it. It should be tended throughout the tow and secured so that it can be released immediately even when under load. A sharp knife should be available in case the line has to be cut in an emergency.

Towing from a quarter cleat sometimes makes it difficult for the boat towing to steer and it may be better to secure a line to both sheet winches which is led aft through the fairleads so that the tow is directly astern.

When the tow is completed, the tow line should be slipped whilst the towed vessel still has sufficient way to reach her berth. Once the tow line has been slipped, the towing vessel should get clear of the path of the towed boat, as it is possible for the towed boat to overrun the other.

If accepting a tow from a powerful motor vessel, it is essential that the towing speed is not so fast that the towed boat becomes uncontrollable, or the attachment points get pulled out of the deck. Power craft often do not appreciate that sailing boats are not designed to withstand being yanked along at speed like a hooked mackerel.

## Mooring end on to a quay (Mediterranean moor)

In countries which have little or no tide and boats moor end on

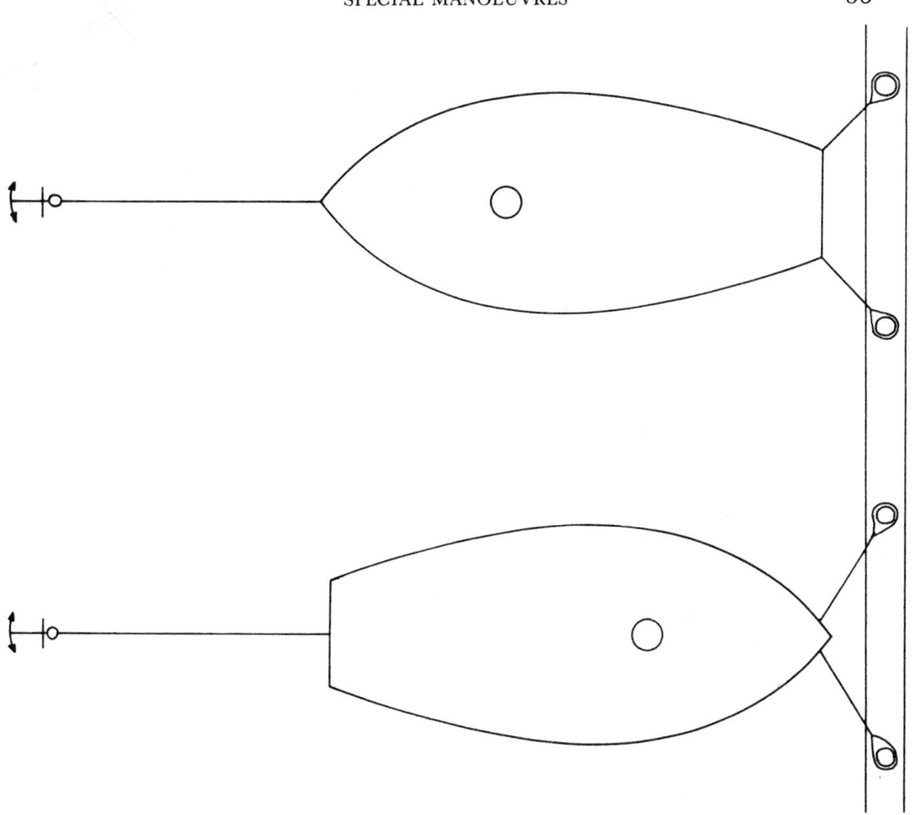

**Fig. 9.1** Two versions of a Mediterranean moor.

to a quay or jetty rather than alongside (Fig. 9.1). The easiest way to do this is to head slowly straight for the quay, drop the kedge anchor three boat's lengths off and motor up to the quay using the kedge as a brake. The crew then jump ashore with lines. The distance off the quay can then be controlled with the kedge line.

It is, however, more seamanlike to go in astern dropping the main anchor from the bows. This manoeuvre can be quite difficult unless well practised. It would be prudent, therefore, to anchor three boats lengths off the quay and then take the lines ashore using the dinghy.

# Part B

*Chapter Ten*

# About Ropes

At one time ropes were made from natural fibres such as cotton, hemp, manila and sisal. Now most ropes are made from synthetic fibres such as nylon, polyester and polypropylene. Synthetic ropes are rot-proof, stronger and lighter than natural fibres of the same diameter, but they can be more slippery and difficult to control.

Synthetic rope can be constructed like traditional rope with three strands (cable laid), or it can be plaited or braided construction (see Fig. 10.1).

*Nylon* is the strongest of the man-made fibres. It stretches and so has good shock-absorbing qualities making it ideal for an anchor warp or mooring line.

*Polyester* is almost as strong as nylon but has low stretching properties making it useful for sheets and halyards. (It is available pre-stretched for this purpose.)

*Polypropylene* is not as strong as nylon or polyester but is lighter and buoyant. So it is useful wherever a lightweight floating line is needed such as a dinghy painter or a line for the lifebuoy.

## Care of synthetic ropes

Wash regularly to remove grit (which can work its way into the rope and cause internal damage) and leave to dry naturally. Excess heat will cause damage. Keep away from corrosive chemicals. Protect from chafe. Mooring lines should be passed through a piece of hose pipe or bound with rag at the point where they go through a fairlead. When ropes such as the main sheet pass around a sheave, the groove in the sheave should be slightly larger than the diameter of the rope. Halyards or sheets may be turned end for end occasionally to spread wear evenly.

## Basic knots, bends and hitches

The term *knot* is generally accepted as meaning any fastening, loop or knob made in cordage. More specifically, a *knot* is a combination of loops used to fasten ropes together or to objects, or to make the end of a rope bigger. A *bend* is a knot used in the joining of two ropes. A *hitch* is a knot which is made up of loops which jam together especially well when under strain but which come apart easily when the strain is removed. Knots, bends and hitches reduce the breaking strain of the rope by as much as 50%.

It is sensible to know the correct knot, bend or hitch for any application, and to be able to tie it quickly and efficiently. Failure to do this could result in loss of the boat or even loss of life.

Figure 10.1 shows types of rope. Figures 10.2 to 10.10 show parts of a rope, useful knots, bends and hitches, and some typical applications.

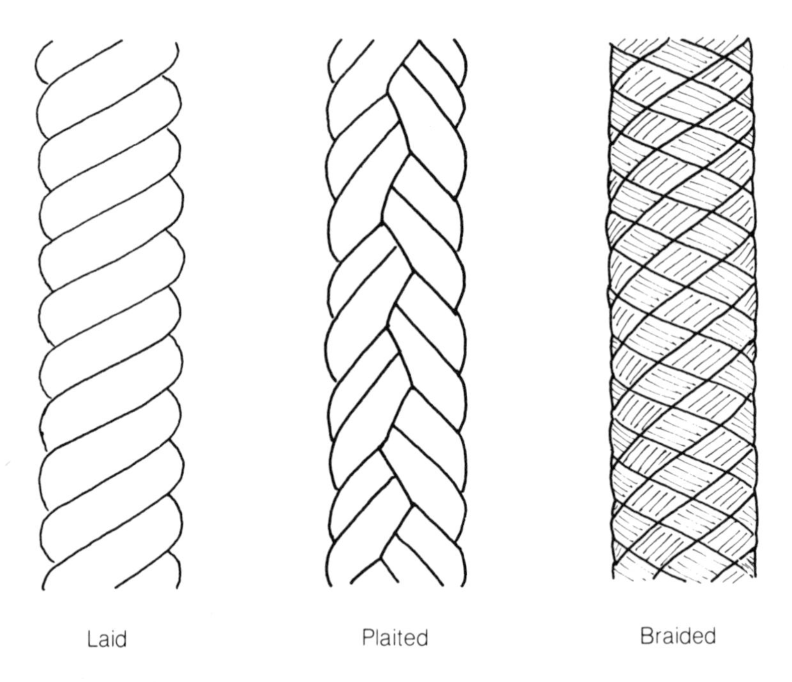


**Fig. 10.1** Types of rope.

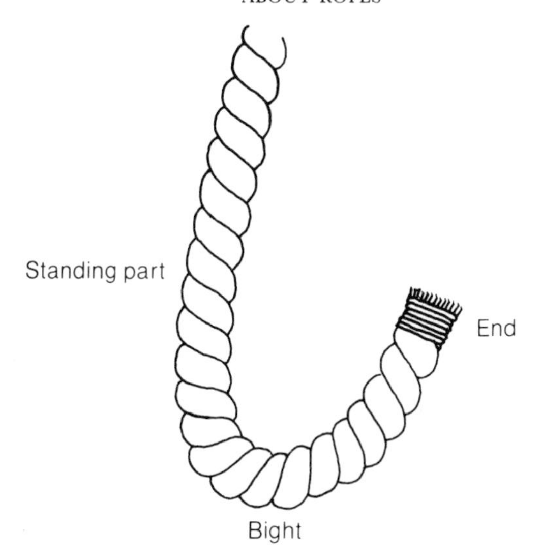


**Fig. 10.2** Parts of a rope.

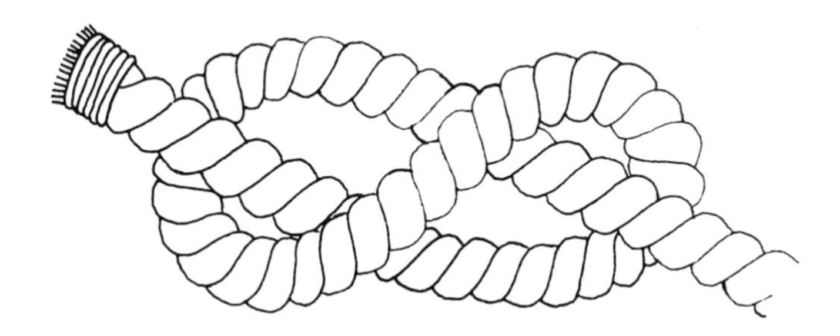

**Fig. 10.3** Figure of eight, sometimes called a stopper knot. It is used on the end of a sheet to stop it accidentally pulling through a block.

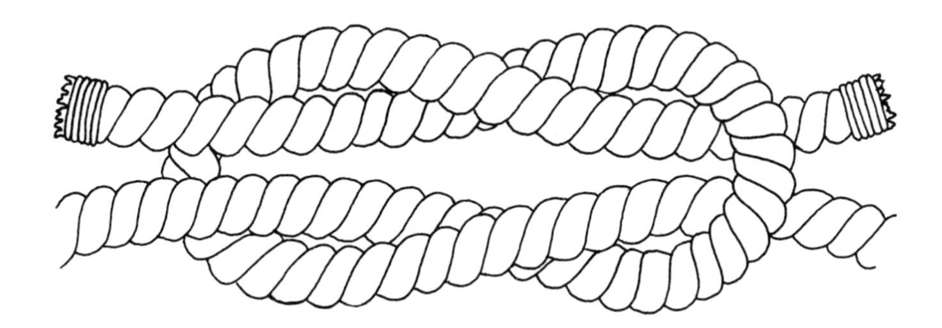

**Fig. 10.4** Reef knot. Used for fastening two ends of the same rope together when reefing a sail.

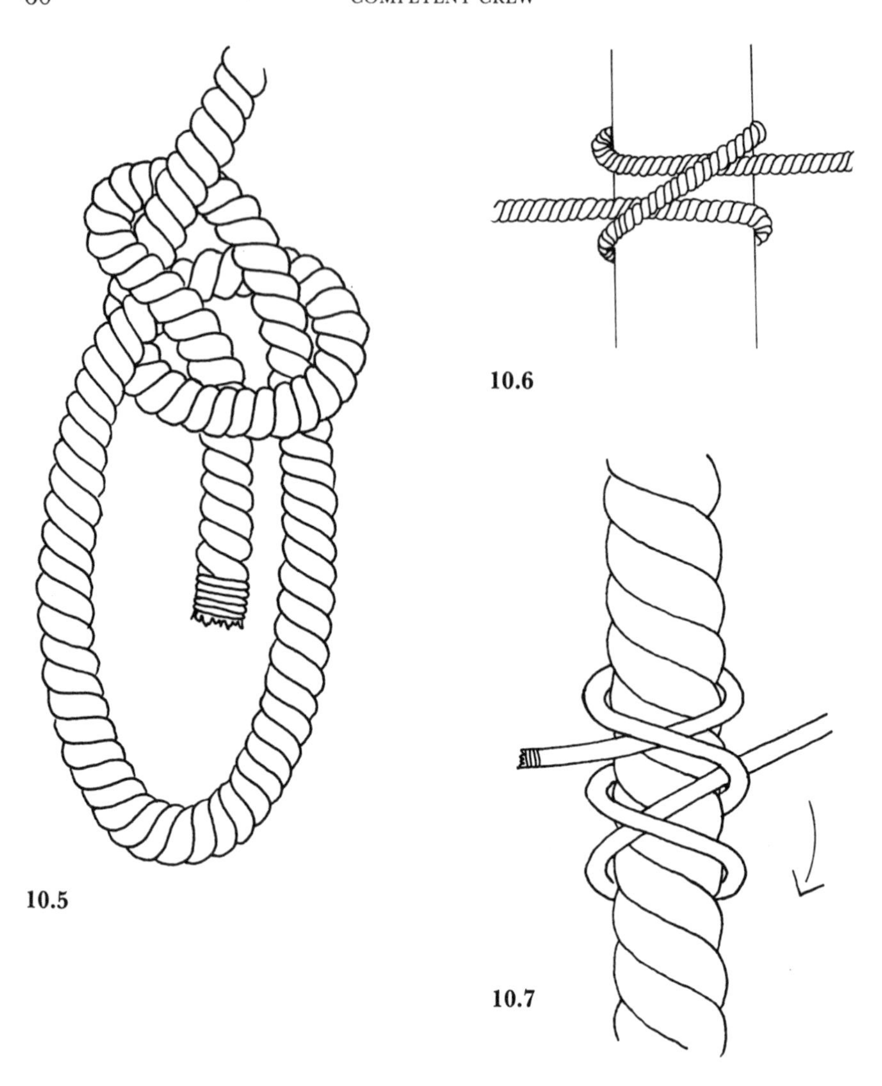


**Fig. 10.5** Bowline. The best all-purpose knot where a temporary loop is required. Some uses are: to fasten the sheets to the headsail; to join two ropes together; to put a temporary eye in a rope.

**Fig. 10.6** Clove hitch. Used to attach the burgee to the burgee pole. Unless under equal tension at both ends this hitch will pull out and so it is unsuitable to use for mooring or for securing fenders permanently.

**Fig. 10.7** Rolling hitch. Used to fasten a rope to a spar, a chain, or a thicker rope to temporarily take the tension. The direction of pull should be lengthwise across the round turn.

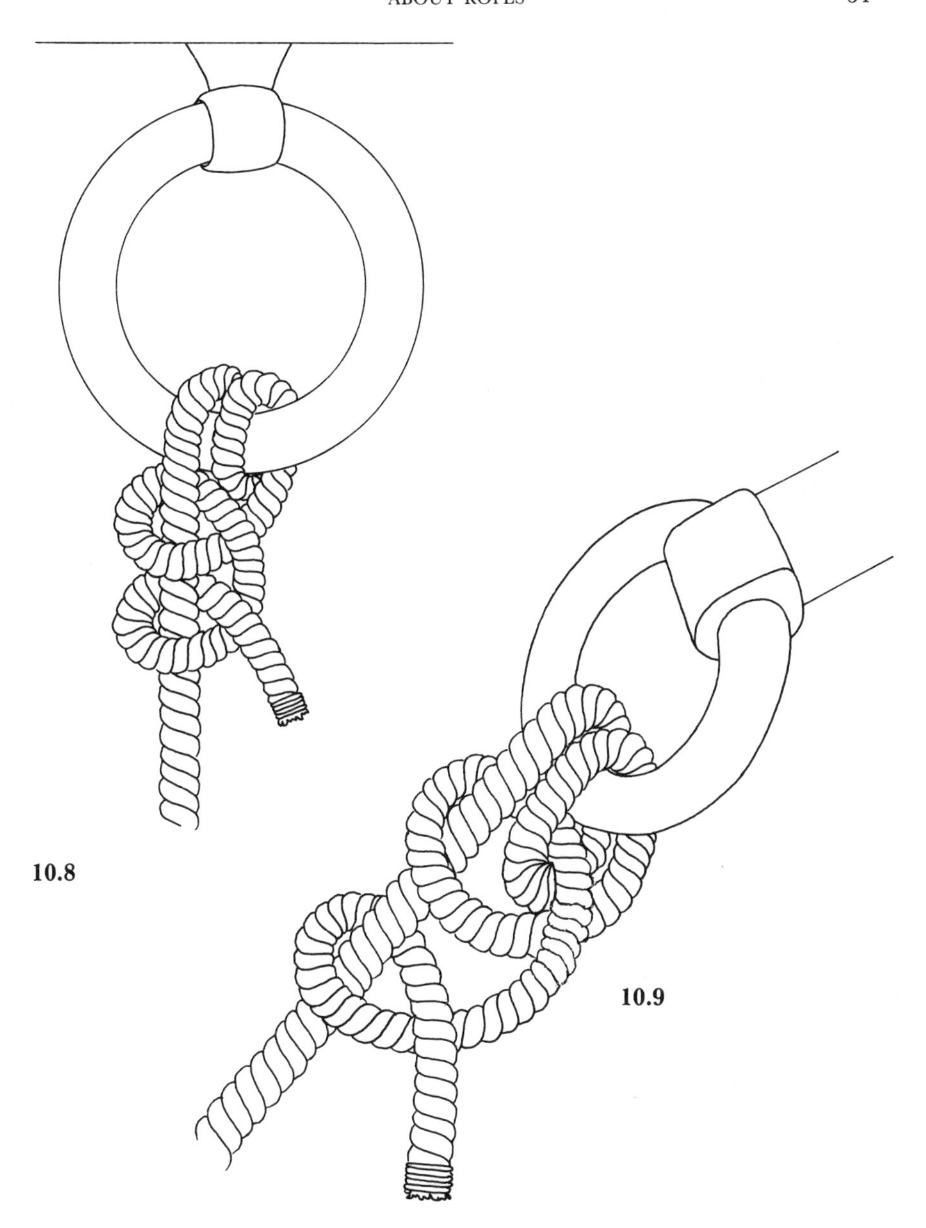


**Fig. 10.8** Round turn and two half hitches. Used for securing a line to a post or ring or for attaching fenders to the boat. It is secure but easy to undo.

**Fig. 10.9** Fisherman's bend. For bending a warp on to the ring on an anchor. It is more secure than a round turn and two half hitches, and holds well on slippery rope.

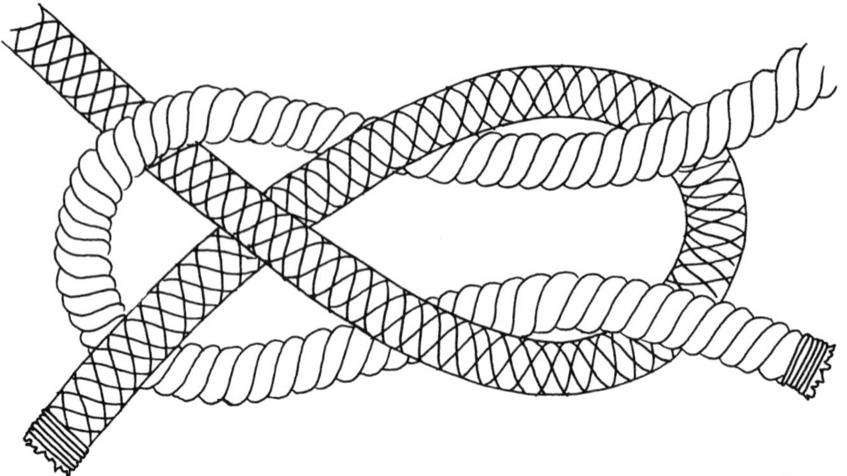

**Fig. 10.10** Sheet bend. For joining two ropes together. The rope can be passed through twice to make a more secure double sheet bend.

## Finishing off the ends

Unless some preventive action is taken, rope ends will sooner or later fray and the rope will unravel. With synthetic ropes, heat sealing is one answer. A hot knife or wire is applied to the end of the rope until the strands melt and fuse together. However, this tends to be a temporary rather than a permanent cure, as eventually the rope will fray again. Another method is to heat shrink a plastic sleeve (these are commercially available) on to the end of the rope. Alternatively, the end of the rope can be woven back into itself, which is called a back-splice (see Fig. 10.13) but this inevitably makes the end of the rope thicker, which could prevent it passing through eyes and blocks; this solution is therefore not favoured by some. The more usual method is to apply a whipping to the rope end (Figs 10.11 and 10.12). There are several different methods.

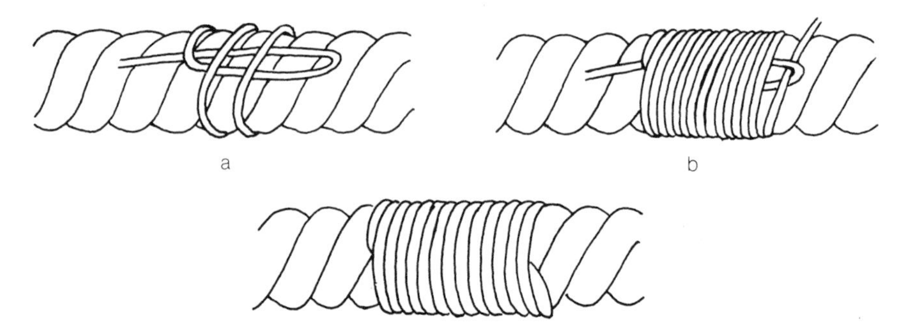


**Fig. 10.11** Common whipping. This is an easy and quick method of finishing off a rope end.

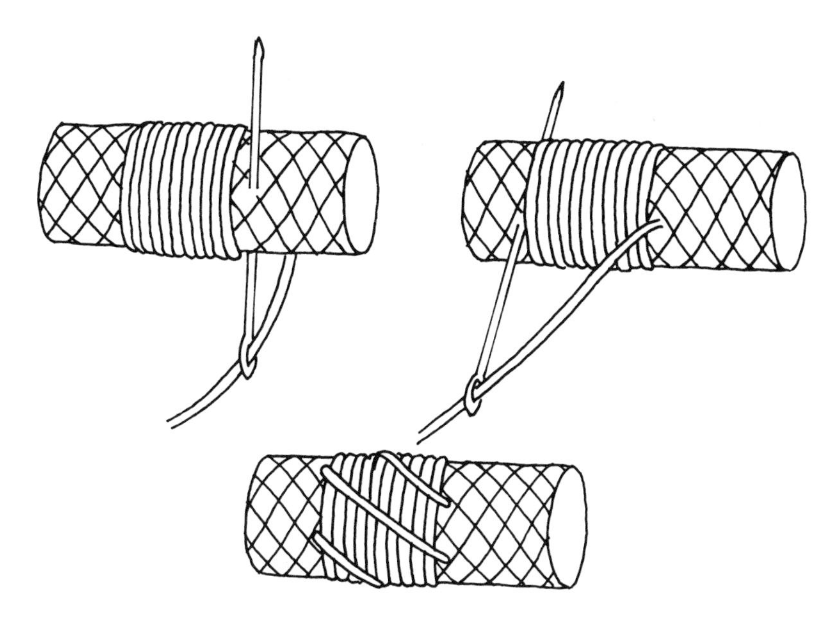

**Fig. 10.12** Palm and needle whipping. This is more secure than Common Whipping. On braided or plaited rope the stitching stops the whipping slipping out of place when the rope stretches.

## Splicing

Splicing is a way of making a permanent eye in the rope, finishing the end of a rope, or joining two ropes together.

### CABLE LAID ROPE (THREE-STRAND)

Splicing this is relatively easy with a little practice. It is useful to have this skill, so that lashings etc. can be replaced if necessary. Figures 10.13, 10.14 and 10.15 show three basic splices.

### BRAIDED AND PLAITED ROPE

Plaited rope (such as Marlow Multiplait) is more complicated to splice than ordinary three-strand rope. Braided rope has an entirely different construction and special methods using appropriate tools are required for splicing. Not many skippers would expect their crew to be expert in this.

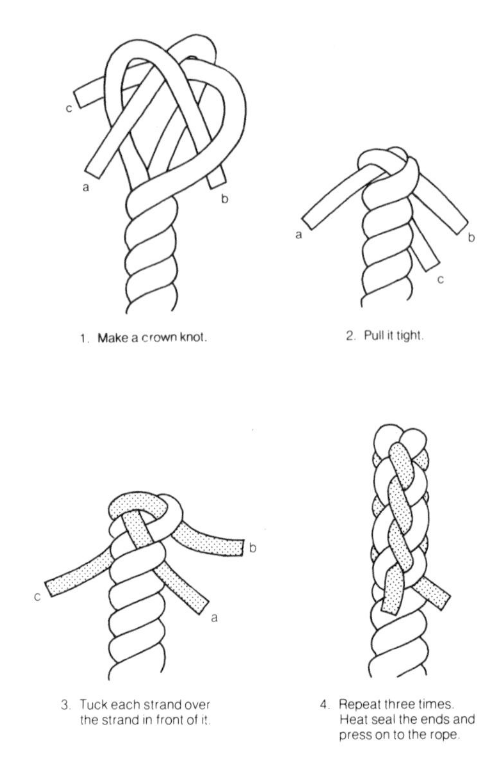


**Fig. 10.13** Back splice. A rope end can be finished in this way to stop it fraying or unravelling but it makes it too bulky to pass through a sheave.

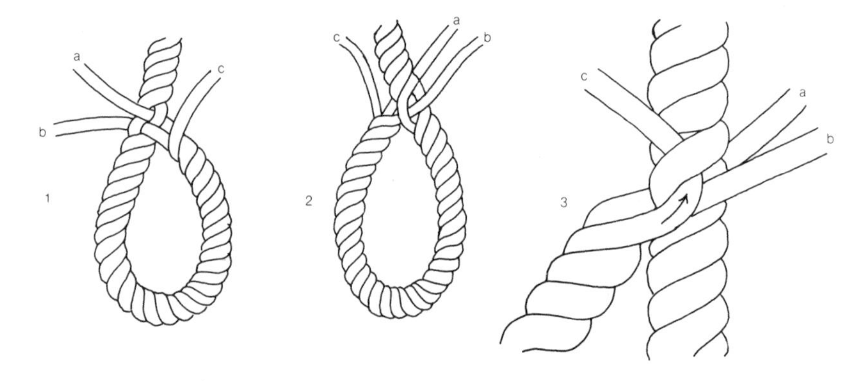


**Fig. 10.14** Eye splice. This splice is used to put a permanent eye in a rope. (1) Tuck strand a under the chosen strand on the standing part of the rope, and strand b under the adjacent left hand strand. (2) Turn the splice over. (3) Tuck strand c from right to left under the strand adjacent to the one used for strand b. (4) Continue as for a back splice until three tucks have been done. (5) Heat seal the ends.

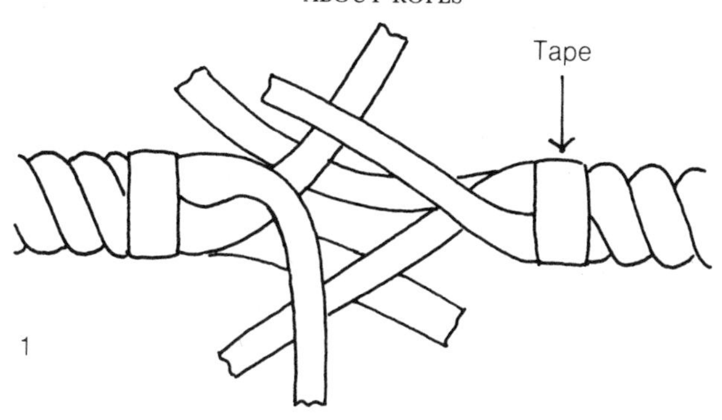


(1) (a) Use tape or twine to stop the rope unlaying. (b) Put the ends together so that opposite strands lie between each other.

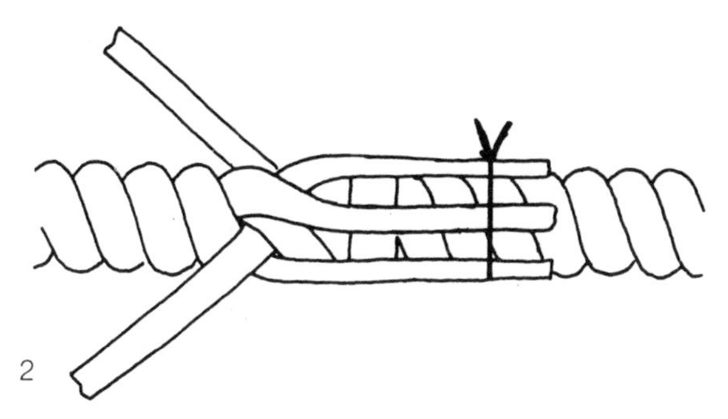


(2) Tape or tie one set of strands. Remove the tape from the opposite rope.

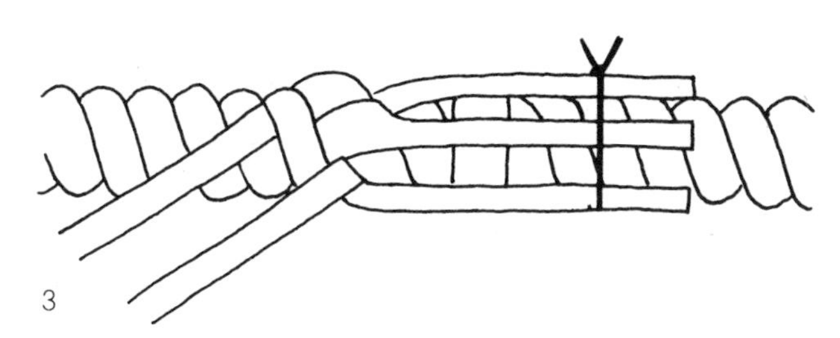


(3) Proceed as for a back splice, tucking the ends under three times. Remove the twine and tape from the other rope and repeat. Heat seal the ends.

**Fig. 10.15** Short splice. This splice is used to join two ropes together.

## Coiling rope

Ropes are normally coiled before being stowed, when preparing to come alongside or for a heavy line (Figs 10.16 and 10.17).

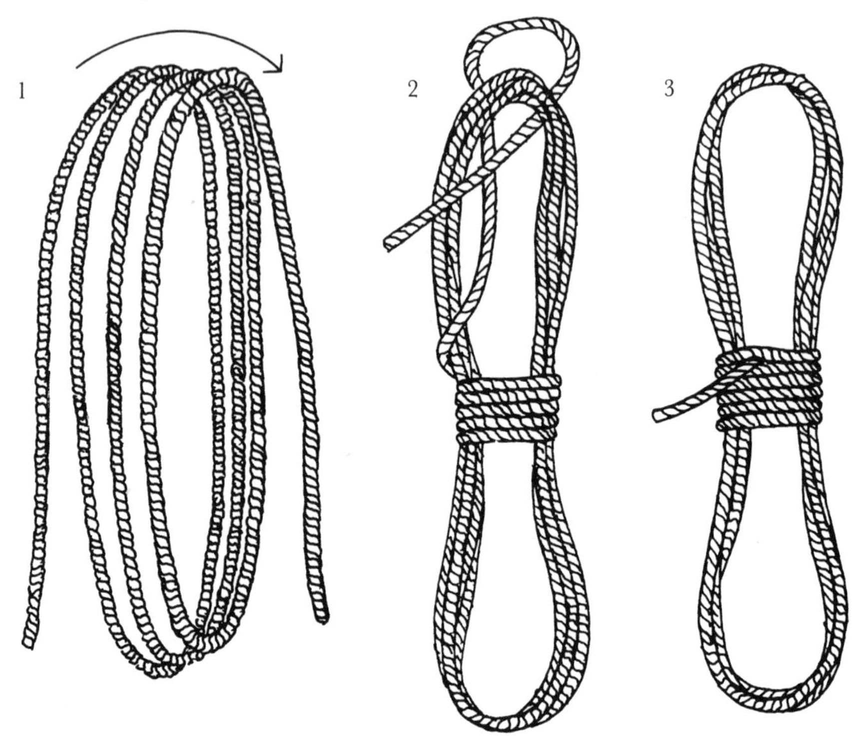


(1) Cable laid rope. Hold the rope in the left hand and coil in a clockwise direction. A twist at the top of each coil stops the rope twisting. (2) Bind the end around the coils several times and then pass a loop through the coils. (3) Bring the loop back over the top of the coils and push it down to the loops binding the coils. Pull the end tight.

**Fig. 10.16** Coiling.

**Fig. 10.17** Coiling. Braided or plaited rope. This type of rope twists if coiled as shown for laid rope. It should be coiled in a figure of eight so that the twists cancel out.

## Winching

A halyard or sheet is turned around a winch drum to take the strain when hoisting or sheeting in a sail. The most important thing to remember when winching is to keep your fingers well away from the winch when there is strain on the rope. The best way to avoid this is to turn the sheet around the winch drum in the manner shown in Plate 1, clenching your fists and keeping them well away from the winch. If the sheet has to be eased out, the palm of the hand should be used (see Plate 2).

**a** Right – the fists are clenched around the sheet and kept well away from the winch drum.

**b** Wrong – the fingers will be trapped against the winch drum.

**Plate 1** Turning a sheet around a winch drum.

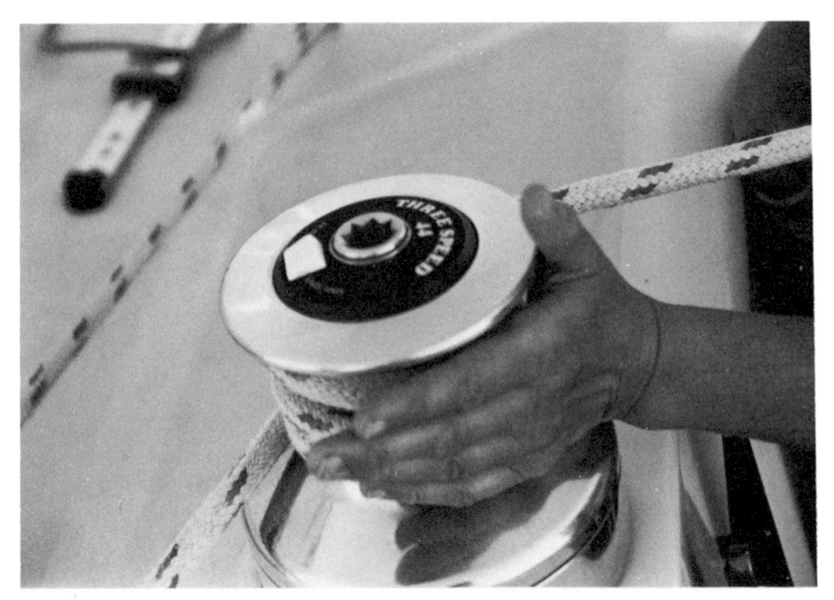


**Plate 2** Easing out a sheet. The palm of the hand is placed against the turns on the drum. The end of the sheet is held in the other hand and the sheet gradually eased out.

To release a sheet lift it above the winch and pull the turns off the top (Fig. 10.18)

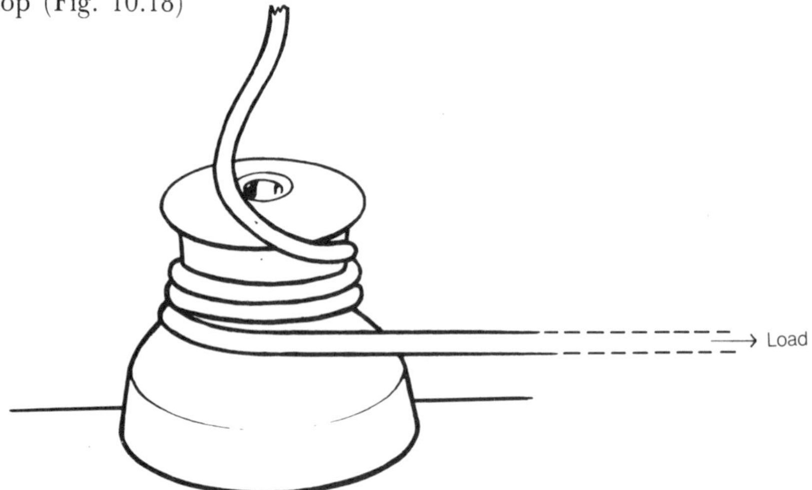


**Fig. 10.18** Releasing a sheet.

A RIDING TURN

Sometimes one turn of a halyard or sheet on the winch drum slips over another and becomes jammed (see Plate 3); this is called a riding turn. It may occur because there are too many turns of rope on the winch drum, or because the lead on to or off the winch is not quite right. They usually free themselves but, if hopelessly jammed, another line must be attached to the halyard or sheet by a rolling hitch (see Fig. 10.7) and the tension taken on this line. With the load off the winch, it is easy to remove the riding turn from the winch drum.

**Plate 3** A riding turn.

## Making up to a cleat

Figure 10.19 shows how a halyard is secured to a cleat. Plate 4 shows a self jamming cleat where it is only necessary to turn the rope once around the cleat to secure it. This type is useful for sheets as it enables them to be released quickly. Plate 5 shows a coiled halyard hung on a cleat.

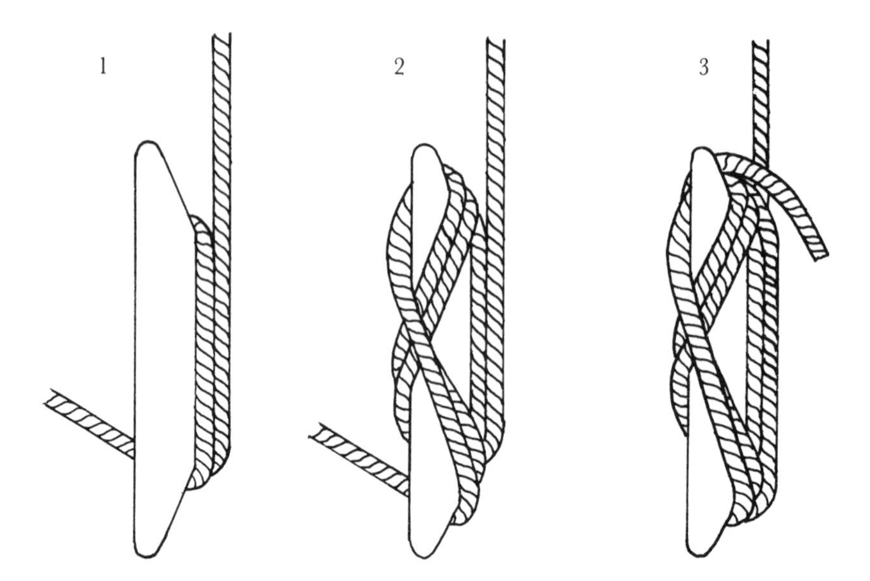


**Fig. 10.19** Making up to a cleat.
(1) Start with a turn around the cleat. (2) Follow with two or three cross turns.
(3) Finish with a round turn to jam the rope.

**Plate 4** A self jamming cleat.

**Plate 5** A coiled halyard hung on a cleat. After cleating a halyard, the remainder is coiled, starting from the end nearest the cleat. About one third of a metre should be left between the cleat and the coil to make a bight in the rope. This is twisted, passed through the coil and looped over the cleat.

## Heaving a line

The line is coiled and the coil divided into two, holding half in each hand as shown in Plate 6. Half the coil is swung backwards and forwards, pendulum fashion, and then thrown (heaved). The other half of the coil is allowed to run free until sufficient has run out and the end of the line has reached its target. The shore end of the line can be made heavier by tying a monkey's fist in the end as shown in Fig. 10.20.

**Plate 6**
A line coiled ready for heaving.

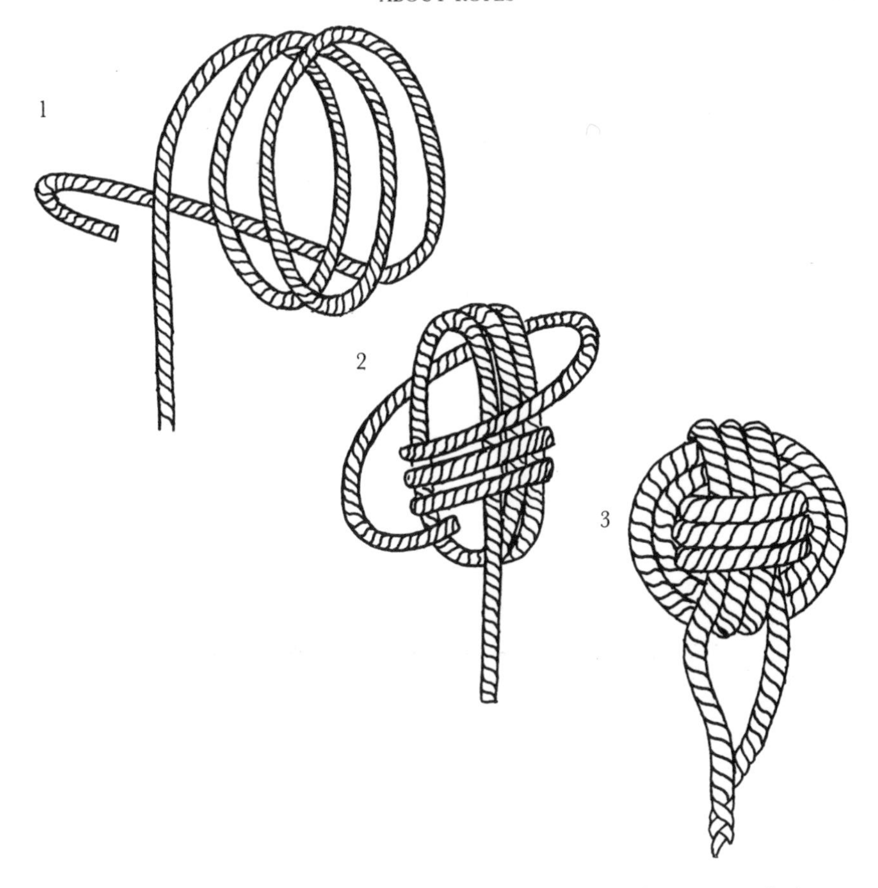


**Fig. 10.20** Monkey's fist. A monkey's fist is made in the end of a rope to make it heavier for heaving. Sometimes it is made around a piece of lead.
(1) Make three loops. (2) Make three more loops outside the first three. (3) Make three final loops over the second three, but inside the first three and splice the end into the standing part.

*Chapter Eleven*

# Weather Wise

*Red sky at night, sailor's delight,*
*Red sky in the morning, sailor's warning.*

*Trace across the sky a painter's brush,*
*The winds around you soon will rush.*

Old sayings, but there is some truth in them. The weather in temperate climates tends to move from west to east. A red sky may be caused by dry air containing dust particles. At sunset this foretells a dry day ahead, whereas at sunrise it means the dry air is moving away and possibly taking with it the fair weather.

The appearance of high cloud called cirrus which looks like wispy threads painted across the sky often occurs before strong winds and bad weather. The towering cumulus cloud in Fig. 11.1 often brings heavy rain and squalls.

The ancient mariner had to rely upon such observations as these. Nowadays with many sources of information on weather available, personal observation tends to be forgotten; but a little time spent looking at the sky can be useful.

**Fig. 11.1** Cumulus cloud.

Most small boats have on board a barometer, which measures atmospheric pressure. Originally many barometers contained mercury and the measurement units were inches of mercury. An *aneroid barometer* does not contain any fluid but works on a vacuum principle, and the measurement unit is a millibar. An aneroid barometer is more suitable for a small boat as a mercury barometer is not accurate if it is shaken about.

The barometric pressure range is normally from a low of 960 millibars to a high of 1040 millibars, the mean being 1000 millibars (one *standard atmospheric pressure*). Changes in barometric pressure can indicate forthcoming changes in weather. Generally, the higher the pressure the more settled the weather and the lower the pressure the more unsettled. Rapidly changing conditions should never be trusted:

Rising rapidly – initially better weather, but it may not be long lasting.
Falling rapidly – bad weather and gales not far off.
Rising steadily – a sign of good weather.
Falling steadily – a sign of bad weather.

So there is some truth in the following rhyme:

*When the glass falls low,*
*Prepare for a blow.*
*When it slowly rises high,*
*Lofty canvas you may fly.*

## Wind

Changes in pressure can result from temperature differences in adjacent regions. Warm air rises causing a low pressure area on the earth's surface; cold air descends causing a high pressure area on the earth's surface. Air tends to flow from a high pressure area to a low pressure area. This movement of air creates wind. Wind force is measured on a scale known as the *Beaufort scale*. Part of this scale (up to force 8) is shown in the table on p. 76.

## Services available

### SHIPPING FORECAST

Weather reports and forecasts are broadcast regularly by the British Broadcasting Corporation and independent broadcasting stations. The principal forecast is the Shipping Forecast which is given on a wavelength of 1500 metres long wave (equivalent to a frequency of

## Beaufort Wind Scale

| *Beaufort Number* | *Mean Wind Speed In Knots* | *Description* | *Sea State* |
|---|---|---|---|
| 0 | Less than 1 | Calm | Sea like a mirror (Fig. 11.2) |
| 1 | 1-3 | Light air | Ripples with the appearance of scales are formed but without foam crests. |
| 2 | 4-6 | Light breeze | Small wavelets, still short but more pronounced. Crests have a glassy appearance and do not break. |
| 3 | 7-10 | Gentle breeze | Large wavelets. Crests begin to break. Foam of glassy appearance. Perhaps scattered white horses (Fig. 11.3). |
| 4 | 11-16 | Moderate breeze | Small waves becoming longer. Fairly frequent white horses. |
| 5 | 17-21 | Fresh breeze | Moderate waves taking a more pronounced long form, many white horses are formed (chance of some spray) (Fig. 11.4). |
| 6 | 22-27 | Strong breeze | Large waves begin to form; the white foam crests are more extensive everywhere (probably some spray). |
| 7 | 28-33 | Near gale | Sea heaps up and white foam from breaking waves begins to be blown in streaks along the direction of the wind (Fig. 11.5) |
| 8 | 34-40 | Gale | Moderately high waves of greater length; edges of crests begin to break into spindrift. The foam is blown in well-marked streaks along the direction of the wind. (Fig. 11.6) |

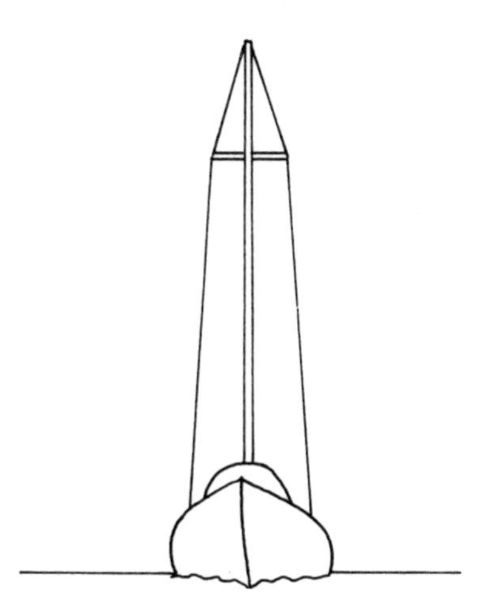

The boat is motoring.

**Fig. 11.2** Beaufort Scale 0.

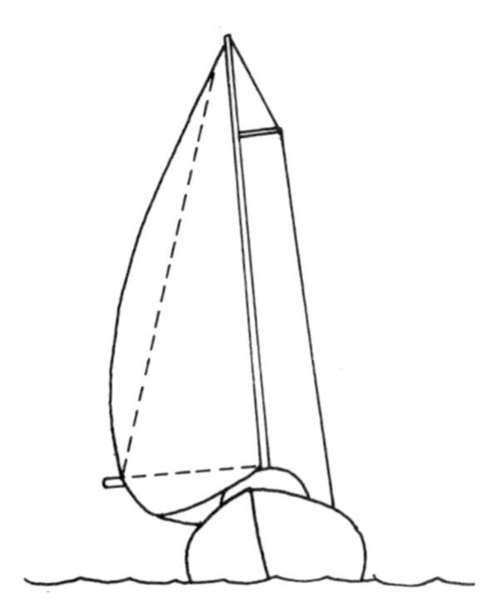

The boat is sailing with a large genoa and full mainsail.

**Fig. 11.3** Beaufort Scale 3.

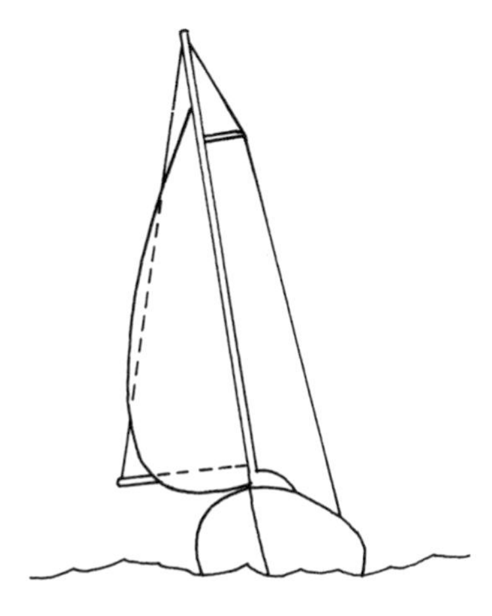

The boat sails well with a working staysail and full mainsail.

**Fig. 11.4** Beaufort Scale 5.

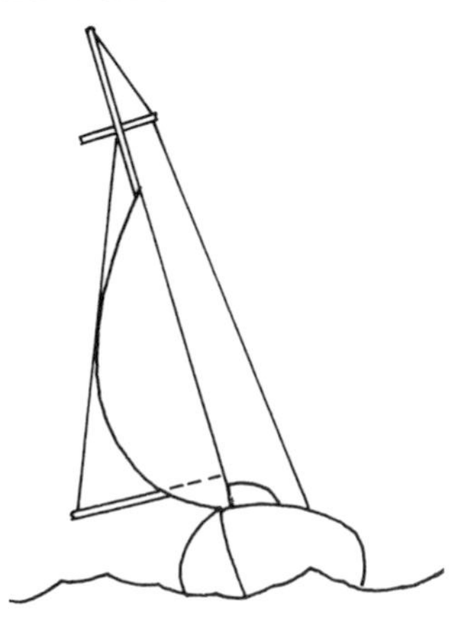

The boat sails with a storm jib and reefed mainsail.

**Fig. 11.5** Beaufort Scale 7.

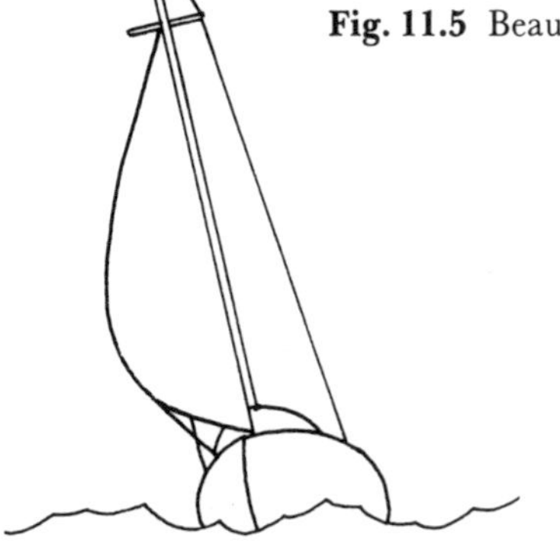

**Fig. 11.6** Beaufort Scale 8.

The boat runs with only a storm jib.

200 kHz) four times a day (at 0033, 0555, 1355 and 1750 clock time). After the 0033 Shipping Forecast, further information is given for inshore waters. After the 1750 Shipping Forecast, a land area forecast is given. The Shipping Forecast includes: any gale warnings in force; the position and probable movement of the various weather systems; a 24 hour forecast for sea areas; and reports from selected coastal weather stations. The Shipping Forecast covers large sea areas so local coastal phenomena may not be included. Some of the terms used in the Shipping Forecast together with their meanings are given below:

*Movement*

Slowly – less than 15 knots
Steadily – 15 to 25 knots
Rather quickly – 25 to 35 knots
Rapidly – 35 to 45 knots
Very rapidly – more than 45 knots

*Pressure changes*

Slowly – less than 1.5 mb in 3 hours
Quickly – 3.6 mb to 6 mb within 3 hours
Very Rapidly – more than 6 mb in 3 hours

*Visibility*

Good – 5 miles to 30 miles
Moderate – 2 miles to 5 miles
Poor – less than 2 miles
Mist or Haze – 1000 to 2000 metres
Fog – less than 1000 metres

*Timing*

Imminent – within 6 hours
Soon – 6 to 12 hours
Later – 12 to 24 hours

## LOCAL RADIO STATIONS

Many local radio stations broadcast local forecasts and often repeat that portion of the Shipping Forecast applying to their local area. A local forecast is useful because it often includes information not in the main Shipping Forecast.

## RECORDED FORECASTS

Pre-recorded forecasts can be obtained on the telephone. These are not necessarily updated to include recent changes in the weather.

### LOCAL FORECASTS

The best source of information for a particular area is from the local weather centre because it will include local conditions not mentioned in the Shipping Forecast.

### COASTGUARD

A weather report can be obtained from the Coastguard by making initial contact on the VHF radio telephone using Channel 16 and then changing to Channel 67.

In many areas the Coastguard broadcasts, on VHF Channel 67 after an initial announcement on Channel 16, regular forecasts covering inshore waters and including strong wind warnings (winds of force 6 or above). These broadcasts include reports from local stations.

### BRITISH TELECOM COAST RADIO STATIONS

Coast Radio Stations broadcast forecasts on local marine band frequencies including any changes that may have occurred since the Shipping Forecast. Gale warnings are included together with the general synopsis from the Shipping Forecast.

### TELEVISION AND NEWSPAPERS

Television and newspapers include a synoptic chart and forecast which can be used to build up a picture of the general weather pattern.

### TIMES OF FORECASTS

Details and times of the various forecasts can be found in: newspapers; nautical almanacs; Admiralty List of Radio Signals; and local nautical publications.

### GALE WARNINGS

When winds of force 8 or above are expected, gale warnings are broadcast on long wave 1500 metres (200 kHz), and they remain in force until amended or cancelled. They are issued at the first programme break after receipt and then repeated after the next news bulletin.

SMALL CRAFT WARNINGS

From April to October when winds of force 6 or more are expected up to 5 miles offshore at any time in the following 12 hours, the Meteorological Office broadcast via both BBC and independent local radio stations a warning for small craft. These broadcasts are made at the first programme break after receipt and repeated after the next news bulletin.

*Chapter Twelve*

# Steering a Course

## The compass course

To steer a course the helmsman uses an instrument called a steering compass. This consists of a bowl filled with liquid which contains a graduated card mounted on a pivot so that it is free to move. Most modern compasses are graduated through 360 degrees. Sometimes the zero may be omitted for clarity (see Fig. 12.1). Magnets attached to the card keep the arrow on the card pointing to the earth's magnetic north pole.

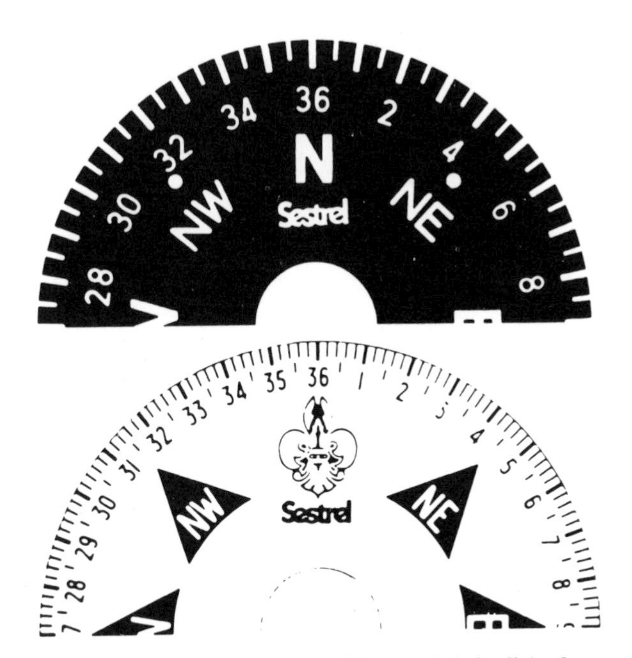


**Fig. 12.1** Two examples of a compass card. The zero is left off the figures for convenience; thus, for example, 34 is 340°, and 4 is 040°.

There is a line on the casing of the compass called a lubber line which is lined up with the boat's fore and aft line when the compass is installed (see Plate 7).

**Plate 7** Sestrel porthole compass from Henry Browne & Son Ltd.

To steer a set compass course, the helmsman must steer so that the lubber line is opposite the desired figure on the compass card. The helmsman should sit directly behind the compass so as to line up the lubber line exactly. As the compass is normally graduated at 5 degree intervals it may be better to steer to the nearest graduation instead of trying to maintain a course somewhere in between. Steering an accurate compass course is not easy and takes some practice, especially in rough conditions.

Because of the influences of the magnetic fields of the earth and also within the boat, the steering compass will not directly indicate true north. However, when plotting a course on a chart, the earth's true north pole is always used as a reference point, so that the charted course is a true course, denoted by the letter T, for example 142° T. Corrections therefore have to be applied to the charted course in order to make it equivalent to the compass course. The correction which has to be applied to compensate for the influence of the earth's magnetic field is called *variation*, and the correction for the boat's own magnetic field is called *deviation*.

## Variation – the influence of the earth's magnetic field

The earth resembles a big magnet with a magnetic field, magnetic meridians and a magnetic north and south pole. The magnetic poles do not coincide with the true geographical poles. The angle between a magnetic meridian and a true meridian is called *variation* (Fig. 12.2). Variation can be either west or east and when applied to the charted course, the resultant course is called a magnetic course, and is indicated by the letter 'M' placed after the figures: 148° M. When correcting a true course to a magnetic course, westerly variation is added and easterly variation subtracted:

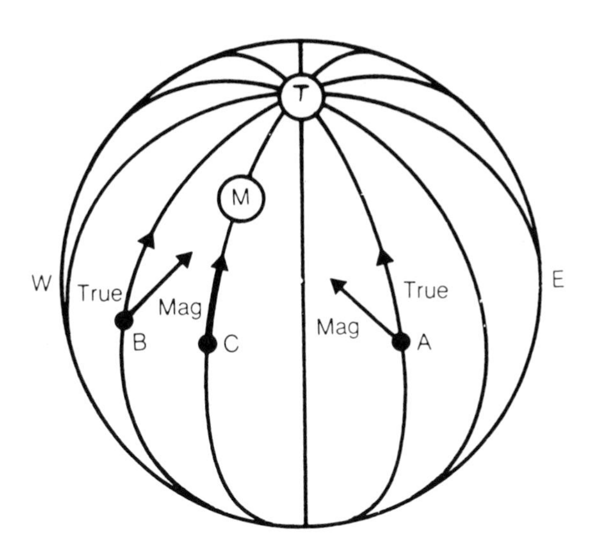


**Fig. 12.2** Variation. Magnetic north M is offset slightly from true north T, so the variation between the two will depend on where you are on the earth's surface in relation to them. At point B variation is East, at A it is West, whilst at C the variation is nil since true and magnetic north are directly in line.

*Example 1*

| | |
|---|---|
| True course | 142° T + |
| Variation 6° west | 6° |
| Magnetic course | 148° M |

Variation differs from one geographical position to another. It also changes slowly from year to year. Variation is printed across the compass rose on any chart (Fig. 12.3). On the compass rose shown, variation is 5°45′W (for 1979) decreasing 4′ annually; so for the year 1985, variation is 5°21′W.

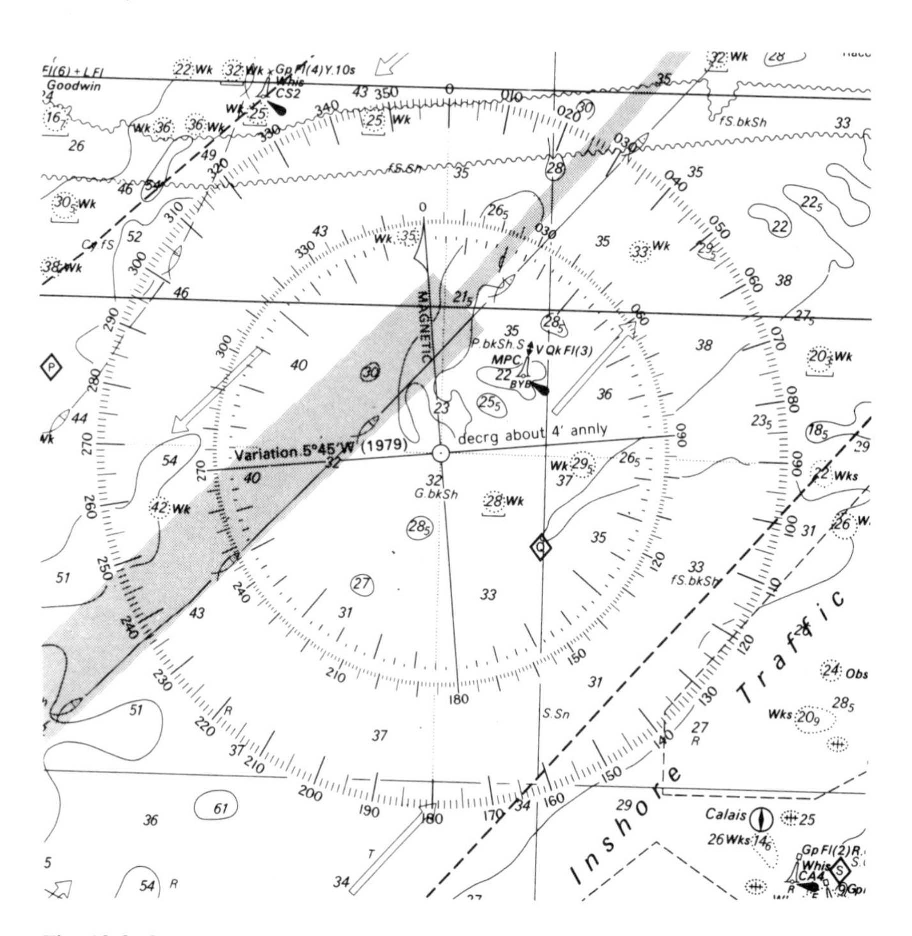


**Fig. 12.3** Compass rose.

## Deviation – the influence of the boat's magnetic field

Ferrous metals, live electrical systems and any equipment containing a magnet may all affect the steering compass and so it is important to site the compass as far away from these influences as possible. The effect on the compass of these influences is called *deviation*.

Deviation alters with different headings of the boat and so a table is necessary to show the correction to apply on the different headings.

One way of making up a deviation table is by the use of landmarks. When two known landmarks are seen from the boat to be in line, they are said to be *in transit*. If the boat is sailed across this transit on a variety of headings, deviation can be determined for each heading. As the boat crosses the transit, the compass bearing of the transit and the heading of the boat are noted using the steering compass. (On most small boats a special attachment called an azimuth ring is needed to enable the steering compass to be used for taking accurate bearings.) The compass bearing of the transit is compared with the magnetic bearing of the transit (found by applying the local variation to the true bearing obtained from the chart). The difference between the compass bearing and the magnetic bearing is the deviation for that course.

Deviation can deflect the compass needle to the west or to the east. When applied to a magnetic course to find the compass course to steer, westerly deviation is added and easterly deviation subtracted:

*Example 2*

| | |
|---|---|
| Magnetic course | 148° M – |
| Deviation 5° East | 5° |
| Compass course | 143° C |

A compass course is indicated by the letter 'C' placed after the figures, for example 143° C.

Temporary deviation can be caused on any magnetic compass by the close proximity of metal objects such as beer cans, penknives, tools and so forth. Always be alert to this danger and keep these objects well away from the compass:

## Taking bearings

A hand held magnetic compass is used to find out the direction of an object on the shore (landmark) from the boat. This direction is called a bearing. Such a compass, called a *hand-bearing compass*, will not be subject to any deviation provided it is held well away from any object on the boat which exerts a magnetic influence. It will, however, still be subject to variation. To take a bearing of a landmark, the compass is held firmly and the 'v' sight aligned with the landmark. When the card stops swinging, the figure under the line on the compass or under the 'v' shaped sight is read: this is the magnetic bearing of the landmark from the boat (see Fig. 12.4).

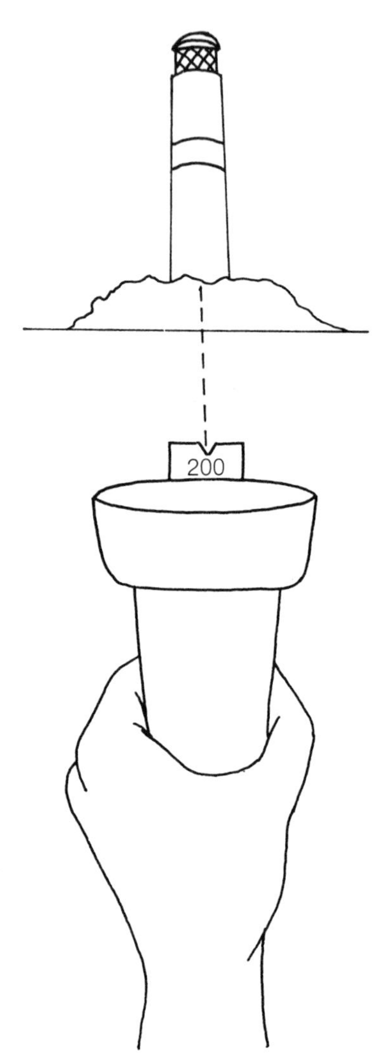


**Fig. 12.4** Taking a bearing with the hand bearing compass.

It is difficult on a rolling or pitching boat to get an accurate bearing as the compass card is very sensitive to movement. The rougher the weather, the more inaccurate the bearing is likely to be. If several bearings are to be taken, those abeam will alter more rapidly than those ahead or astern so they should be taken last.

Always note the time at which bearings are taken, and the log reading if appropriate.

*Chapter Thirteen*

# Finding the Way

Charts are nautical maps. A *pilot* (also called *sailing directions*) is a book which gives detailed information about harbours, anchorages, the coastline, tidal conditions, local weather patterns and so forth.

The theory of coastal navigation, such as plotting on the chart, can be learned on a shorebased course over the winter. It is useful for crew members to have an understanding of pilotage which is navigating with the use of floating marks (called buoys) or other land features such as lighthouses, beacons, towers or churches, where the next mark on the passage can be seen at all times.

It is essential to learn to recognise the various marks both by day and by night; and to locate their positions on the chart.

## Buoyage

The system of buoyage around North West Europe has been developed by the International Association of Lighthouse Authorities and is called IALA System A. (IALA System B applies around North America.)

### LATERAL MARKS

A lateral mark indicates the port or starboard side of a channel when used in relation to the Conventional Direction of Buoyage. The Conventional Direction of Buoyage (which is shown by a broad arrow on large scale Admiralty charts) is usually in a clockwise direction around land masses, or in the general direction of approach from seaward when entering a harbour, river or estuary (Fig. 13.1)

When proceeding in this direction, red cylindrical marks are left to port and green conical marks are left to starboard. Their shapes may vary (see Figs 13.2 and 13.3). Lateral marks do not always carry topmarks.

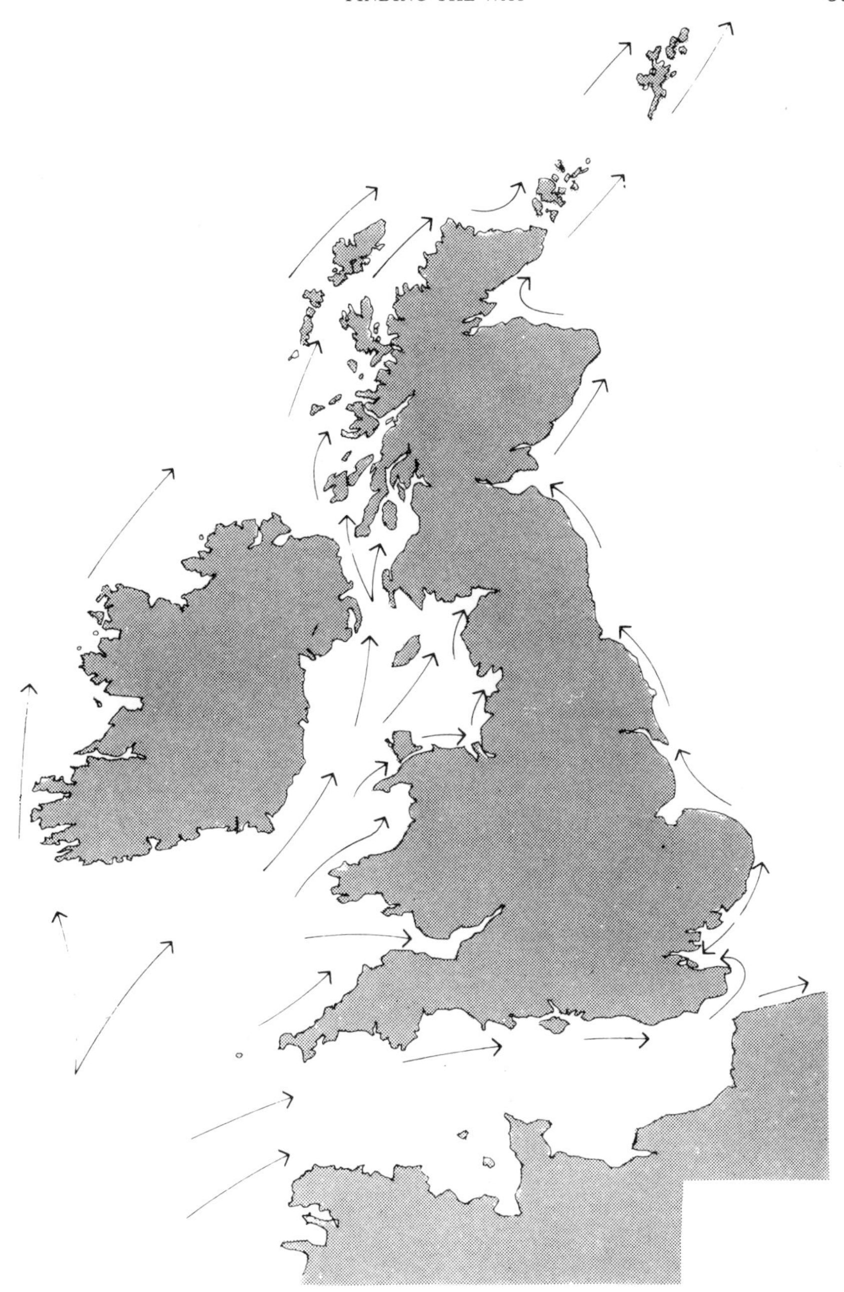

**Fig. 13.1** The Conventional Direction of Buoyage in the British Isles follows the arrows shown.

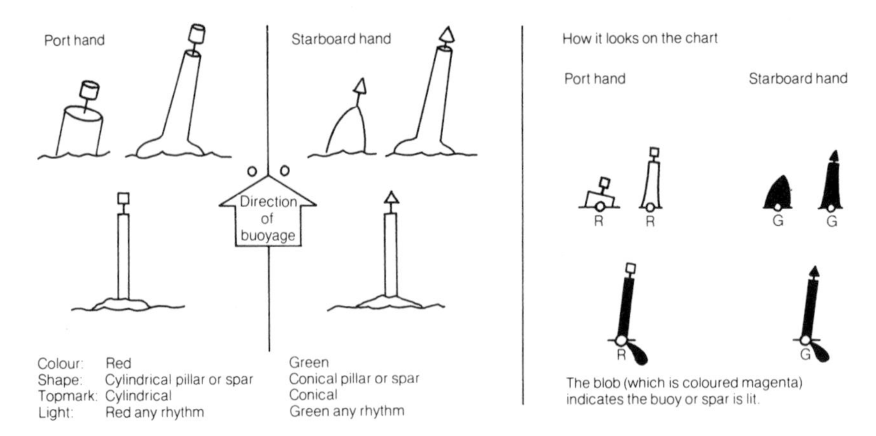


**Fig. 13.2** Lateral marks.

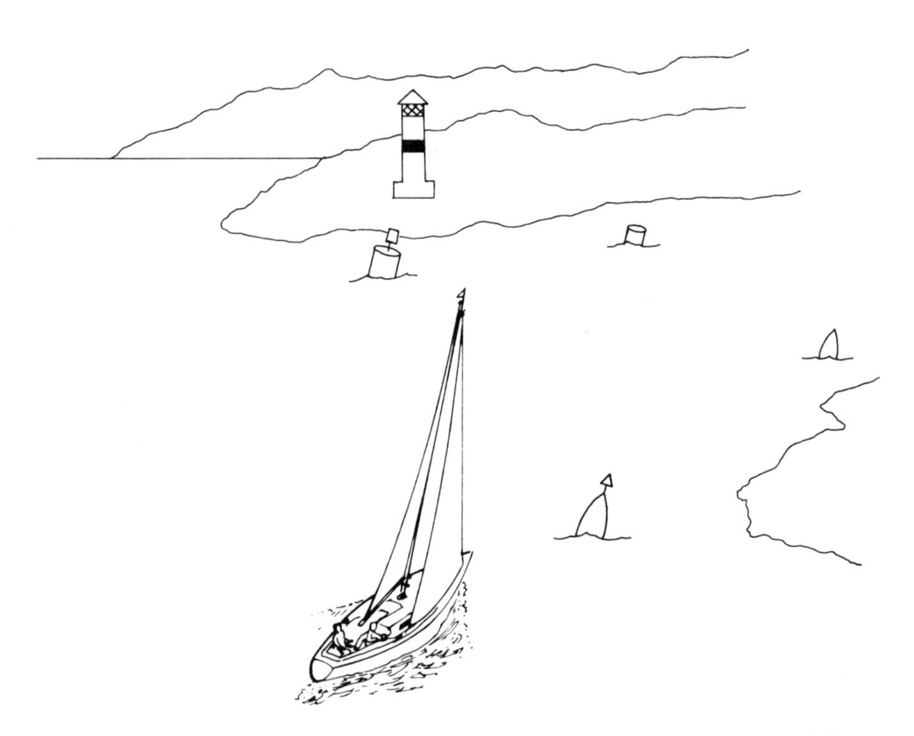

**Fig. 13.3** When entering a harbour the red port hand marks are left to port and the green starboard hand marks to starboard.

Where the channel divides, the lateral marks are modified by a green or red horizontal band which indicates the main or preferred channel (Figs 13.4 and 13.5).

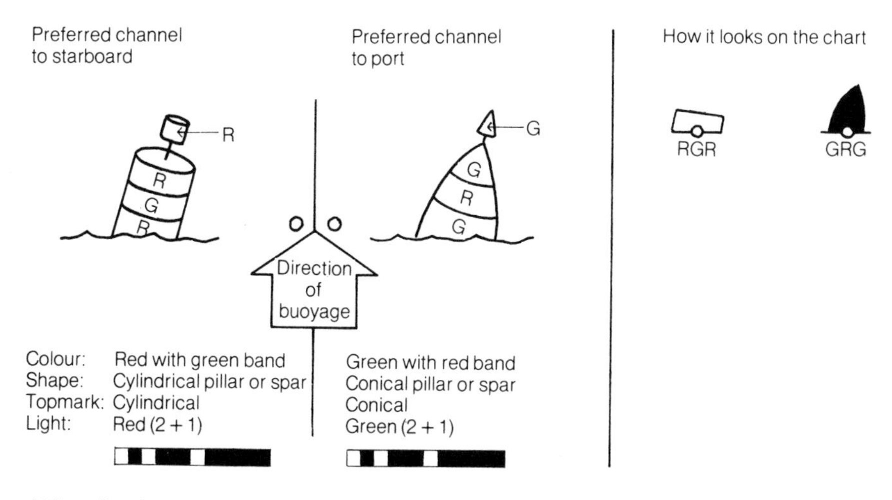


**Fig. 13.4** Preferred channel marks.

**Fig. 13.5** Although the main channel is to starboard, this yacht is sailing up the secondary channel to her mooring up the creek.

### CARDINAL MARKS

Cardinal marks are pillar shaped, with black and yellow horizontal bands and black topmarks. They are placed north, south, east or west of the danger which they mark, and it is easy to remember which particular mark you are looking at (you have to know which side of it to go) if you note that the topmarks point upwards for the north mark, downwards for the south mark, make an *e*gg shape for the *e*ast mark, and a *w*ineglass shape for the *w*est. If you cannot see the topmark properly, the placing of the black band in fact corresponds to the way the topmarks point. As for the lights, the number of flashes corresponds to the mark's 'clockface' position (see Figs 13.6 and 13.7).

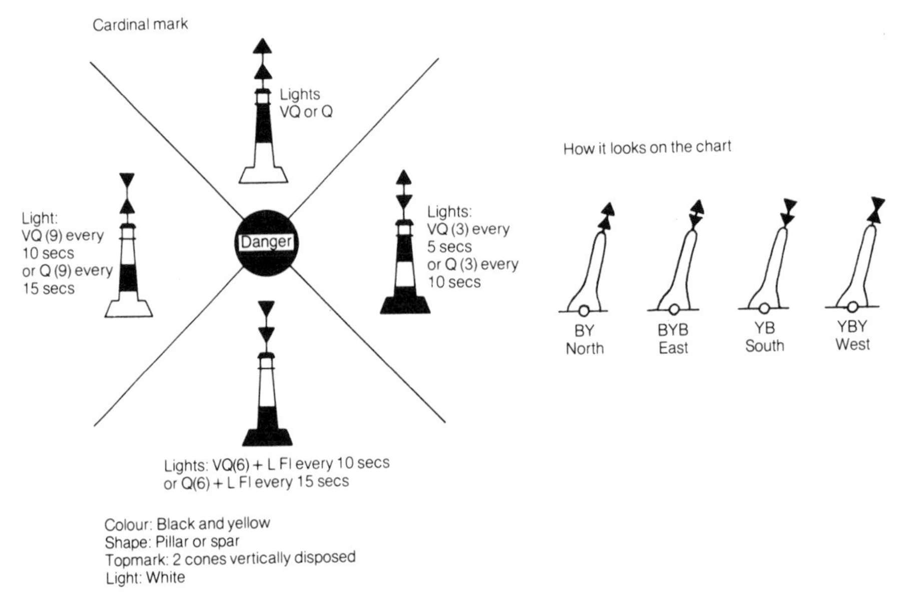


**Fig. 13.6** These marks are positioned to the north, east, south or west of danger.

### ISOLATED DANGER MARKS

Figure 13.8 shows an Isolated Danger mark which is placed immediately over the underwater obstruction.

### SAFE WATER MARKS

A Safe Water mark indicates safe water all around it. It may be used as a landfall mark or a mid channel mark (Fig. 13.9).

### SPECIAL MARKS

A special mark has no navigational significance but indicates a

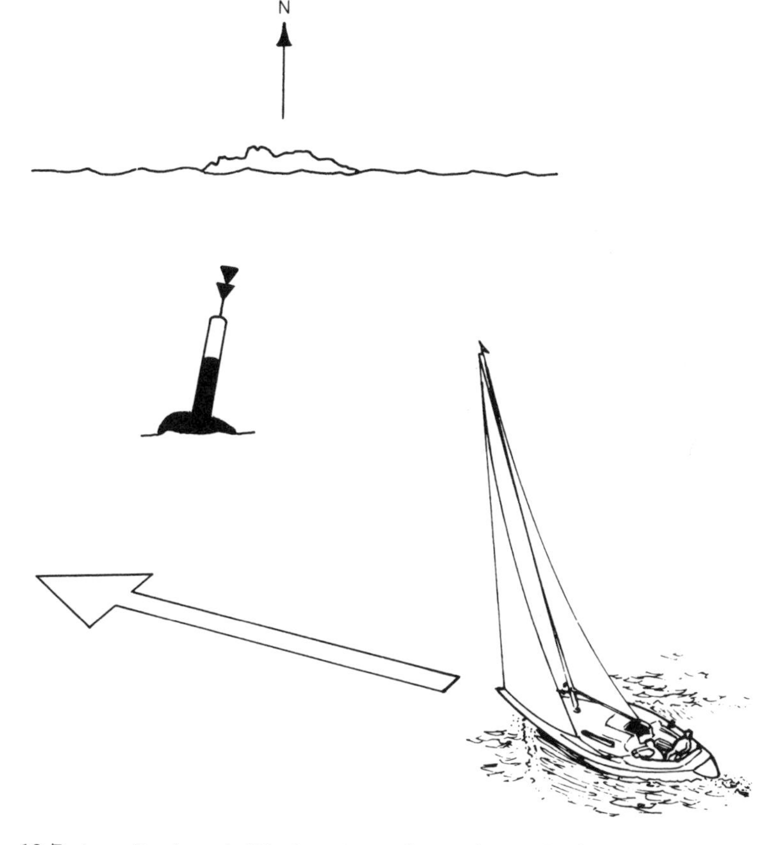


**Fig. 13.7** A cardinal mark. The boat is passing to the south of the SOUTH cardinal mark to avoid the rock to the north of the mark.

Colour: Red and black horizontal bands
Shape: Pillar or spar
Topmark: 2 spheres vertically disposed
Light: White, group flashing (2)

This mark is over an isolated danger where there is navigable water all around it.

**Fig. 13.8** Isolated danger mark.

special feature such as a traffic separation scheme, spoil grounds, or a military exercise area (Fig. 13.10).

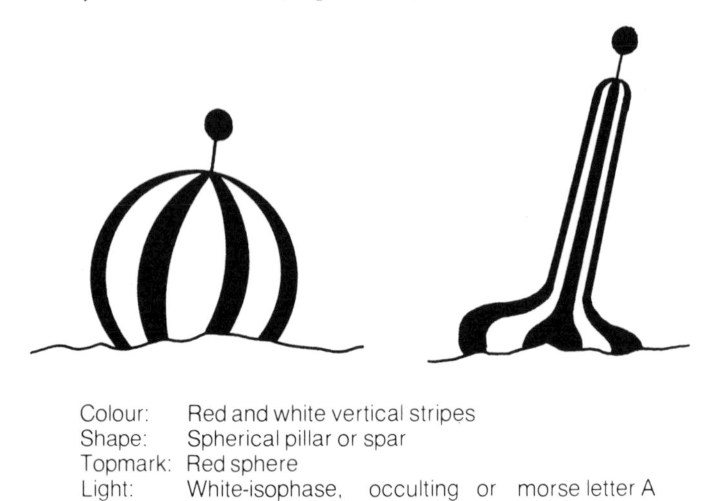

Colour: Red and white vertical stripes
Shape: Spherical pillar or spar
Topmark: Red sphere
Light: White-isophase, occulting or morse letter A

How it looks on the chart

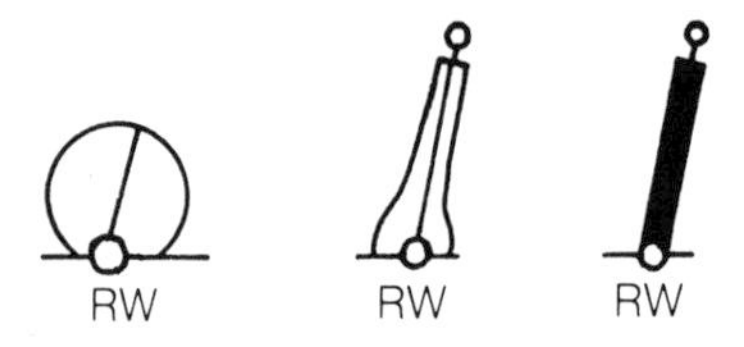


This mark indicates that there is safe water around it.

**Fig. 13.9** Safe water mark

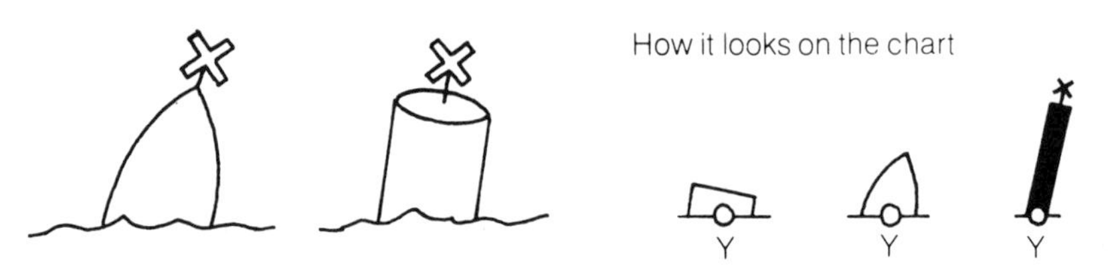


Colour: Yellow
Shape: Optional
Topmark: Cross
Light: Yellow

These are not navigational marks but have a special meaning which may be indicated on the chart. The shape is optional but must not conflict with navigational marks in the area.

**Fig. 13.10** Special mark.

## Shore lights

In addition to buoys, lighthouses and beacons on the shore are used to determine the boat's position by day; or by night when they are identified by lights with specific characteristics.

## Light characteristics

Lights used for navigation operate on a regular cyclic period during which they exhibit specific identification characteristics. Figure 13.11 shows some light characteristics. Figure 13.12 shows sectored lights.

### PERIOD

The period is the time in seconds that a light takes to exhibit its complete characteristics, which includes the time that it is eclipsed.

It is a good idea, when trying to identify a light, to use a stopwatch to time the period. It is easy to imagine that the characteristics match those of an expected light and thus make a wrong identification.

## Transits

Two shore objects or lights in line are often used to enter a harbour or river. When they are in line they indicate the safe route to be followed. Such marks are called leading marks or transits (Fig. 13.13)

## Clearing bearings

Sometimes specific bearings or transits are used to ensure that the boat stays in a safe area (Fig. 13.14).

## Withies

Further up the river or creek, the navigational marks may consist only of tree branches or sticks stuck into the mud, marking the edges of the navigable channel. These are called withies, and are not painted any colour (see Fig. 13.15)

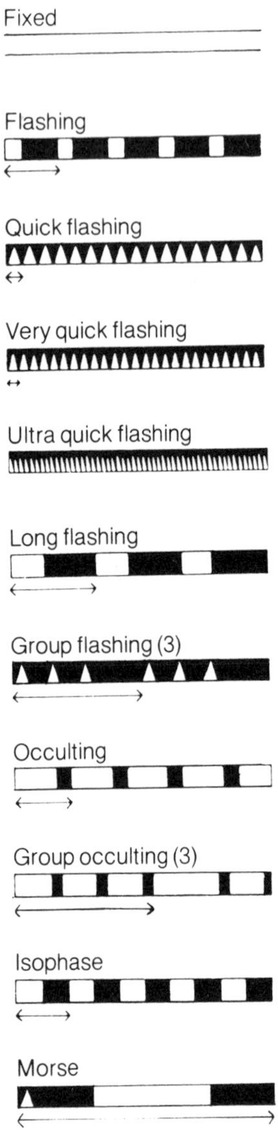

| | |
|---|---|
| Fixed | Fixed (F). A light which is on all the time. |
| Flashing | Flashing (F1). The dark period exceeds the light period. |
| Quick flashing | Quick Flashing (Q). 50-79 flashes per minute. |
| Very quick flashing | Very Quick Flashing (VQ). 80-159 flashes per minute. |
| Ultra quick flashing | Ultra Quick Flashing (UQ). 160 or more flashes per minute. |
| Long flashing | Long Flashing (LF1). Flash 2 seconds or longer. |
| Group flashing (3) | Group Flashing (F1). A number of flashes within a certain time period: F1 (3). |
| Occulting | Occulting (Oc). The light period exceeds the dark period. |
| Group occulting (3) | Group Occulting (Oc). A number of occults within a certain time period: Oc (3). |
| Isophase | Isophase (Iso). The periods of light and dark are equal. |
| Morse | Morse (Mo (A)). Shows a morse letter (in this case 'A'). |

**Fig. 13.11** Light characteristics.

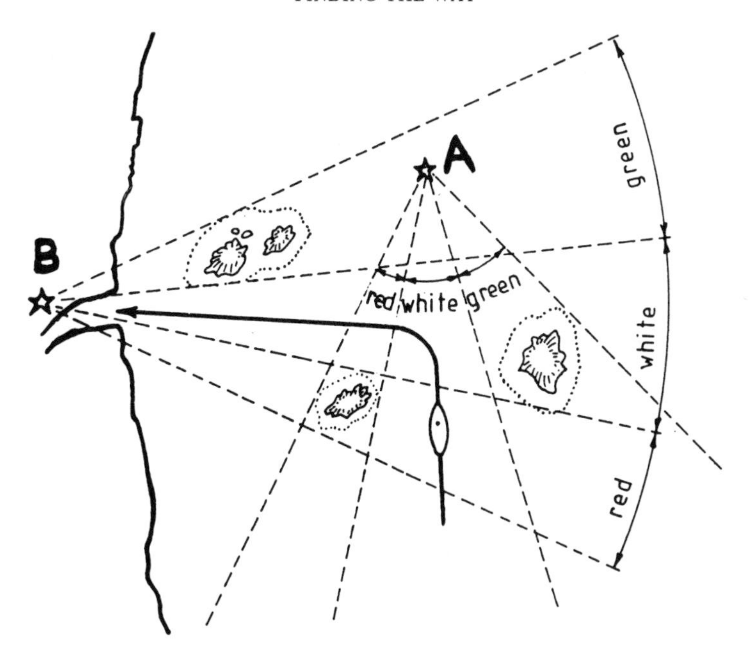


**Fig. 13.12** Sectored lights. Many lights have sectors of different colour: here the vessel must keep in the white sector of light A until she reaches the white sector of light B, when she can turn to port.

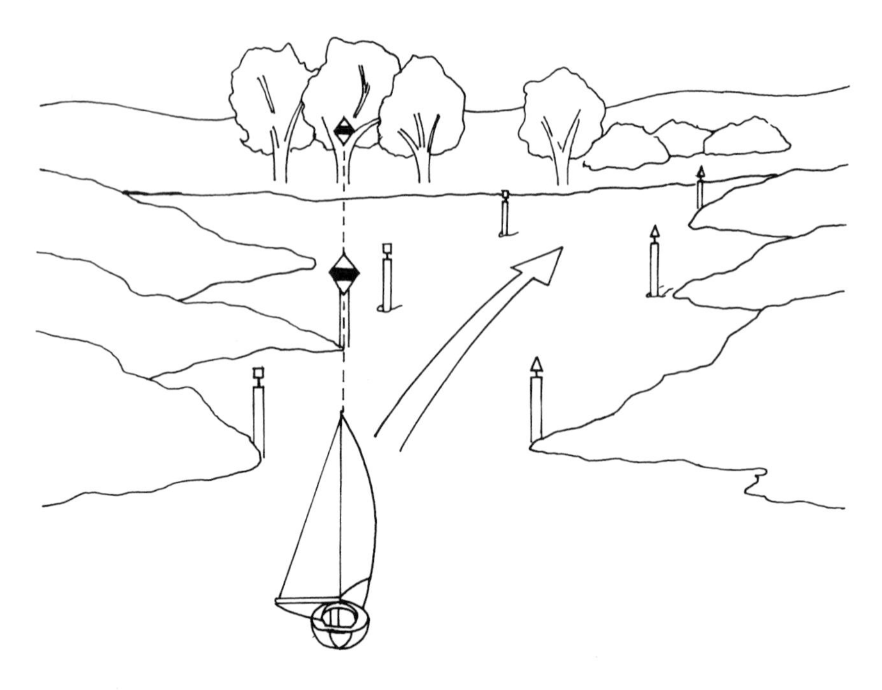

**Fig. 13.13** A transit. The boat lines up the diamonds to enter the river and then keeps between the port and starboard marks.

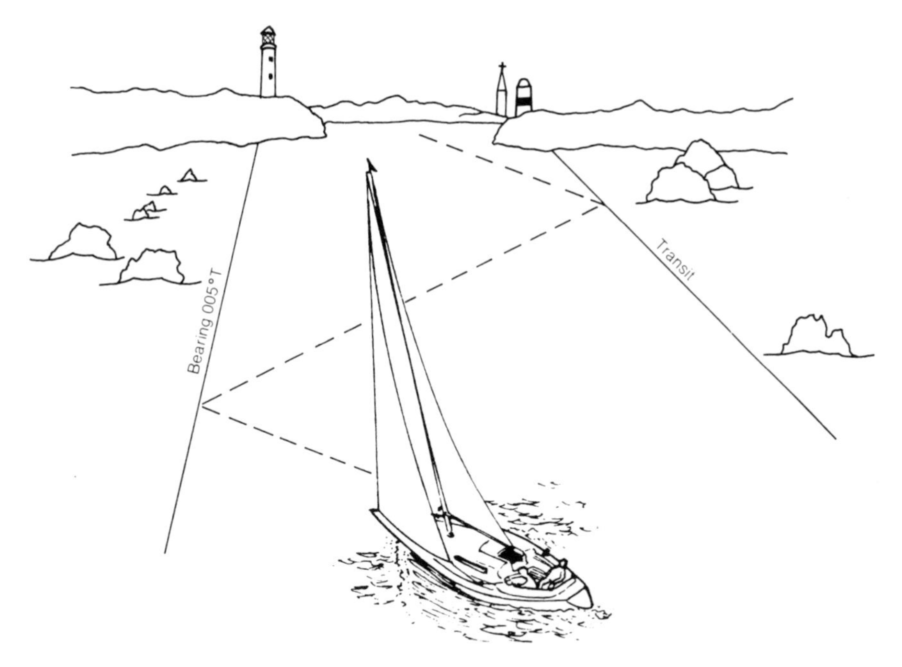


**Fig. 13.14** Clearing bearings. The boat uses clearing bearings to stay in safe water. She alters course when the lighthouse bears 005° T and again when the church and the beacon are in transit.

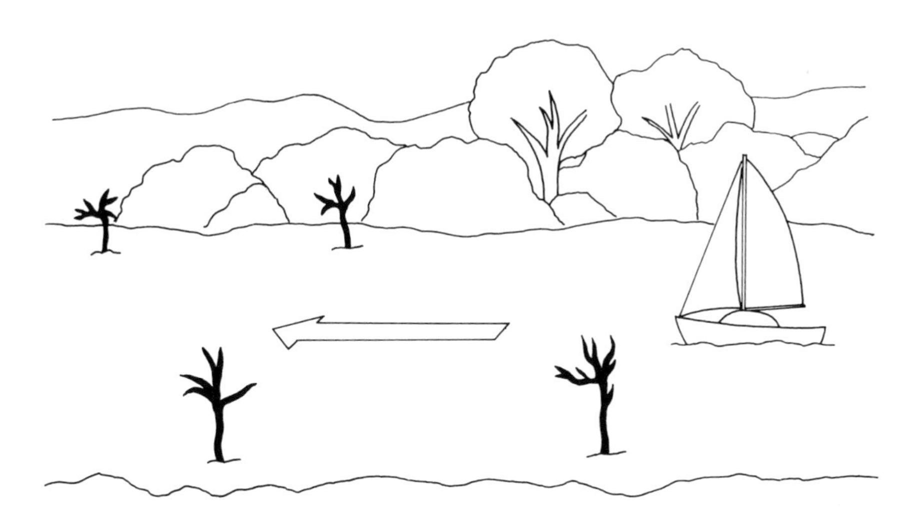

**Fig. 13.15** Withies. Further up the river, tree branches may be stuck in the mud to mark the edge of the channel. These are called withies.

*Chapter Fourteen*

# Who Goes First?

Just as there is a code on the highway to ensure the safety of road users, so there are rules to ensure the safety of seafarers. At sea these rules are called the International Regulations For Preventing Collision At Sea. Every yachtsman should have a thorough knowledge of the principal rules and at least a working knowledge of the remainder. Those concerning small sailing and power driven vessels are discussed here but a full copy of the rules should be studied in conjunction with this chapter.

## Keeping a good lookout

This is probably the most important rule as collisions cannot be avoided unless the danger of collision has been observed. A proper lookout must be kept *at all times* not only by watching but by listening, especially if visibility is poor. In a sailing boat which is heeling over, the crew must be particularly observant to leeward as the headsail can obscure the helmsman's vision in this direction (Fig. 14.1)

## Is there a risk of collision?

A compass bearing is taken of a boat suspected to be on a collision course. Further bearings are taken at regular intervals. If there is little or no difference between these bearings, then a risk of collision is deemed to exist (Fig. 14.2).

## Avoiding action

Avoiding action should be: a *positive* alteration of course made in ample time and with due observance of the rules of good seamanship. A positive alteration of course is about 40 degrees:

**Fig. 14.1** Keep a good lookout especially to leeward.

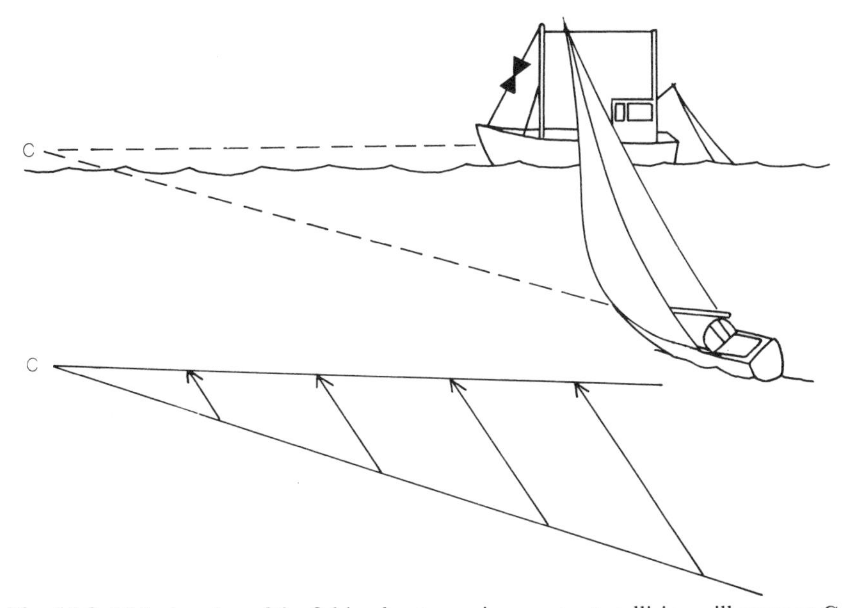


**Fig. 14.2** If the bearing of the fishing boat remains constant, collision will occur at C.

ample time (for a sailing boat) is about 5 minutes: and good seamanship is not crossing ahead of another vessel. A boat should always travel at a safe speed relative to the prevailing weather conditions and traffic density, so that action taken to avoid collision can be made in good time. This may mean slowing down if there is bad visibility when there are other boats in close proximity, or speeding up (by using the engine) if there is little or no wind near a harbour entrance or in a shipping lane (a sailing boat is required to start its engine if travelling at less than 3 knots when crossing a shipping lane).

## Narrow channels

In narrow channels boats must keep over to the side of the channel which is to their starboard. Sailing boats and boats of less than 20 metres in length must not impede the passage of a vessel using the channel which can only navigate within that channel. If crossing the channel this should be done at right angles. If there is sufficient depth of water outside the main channel the smaller boat should stay out of that channel.

When approaching the bend in a river which obstructs a clear view, a boat should sound one long blast on a siren or foghorn and listen for a reply (Fig. 14.3).

A boat should not anchor near or in a channel.

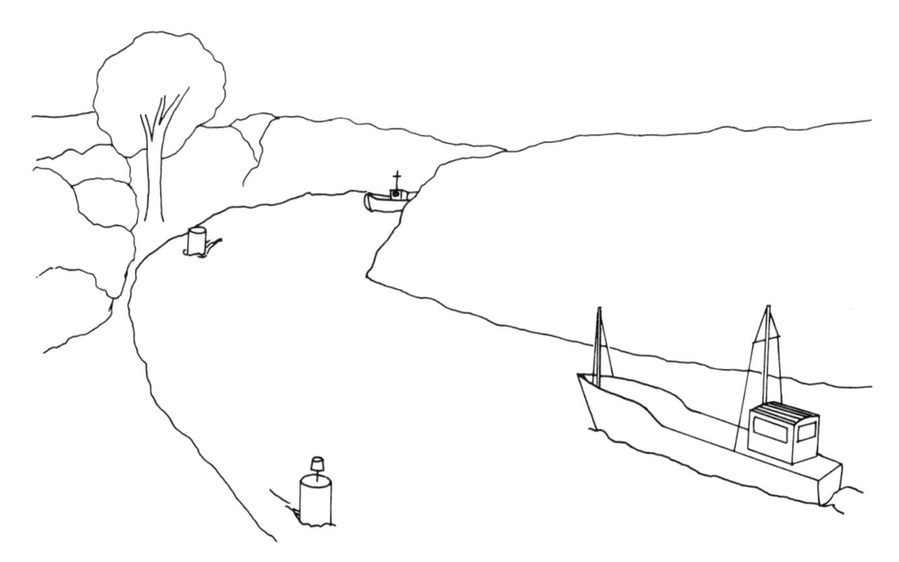

**Fig. 14.3** Approaching the bend in the river, sound one long blast and listen.

## Crossing a traffic separation scheme

Around headlands or in channels where there is much shipping, larger vessels are confined to special traffic lanes which are marked on the chart. If a boat has to cross a traffic lane then she must do so at right angles as quickly as possible (Fig. 14.4). When so crossing, it is the heading of the boat that should be at right angles to the traffic lanes, and not the ground track (which will be affected by any tidal stream).

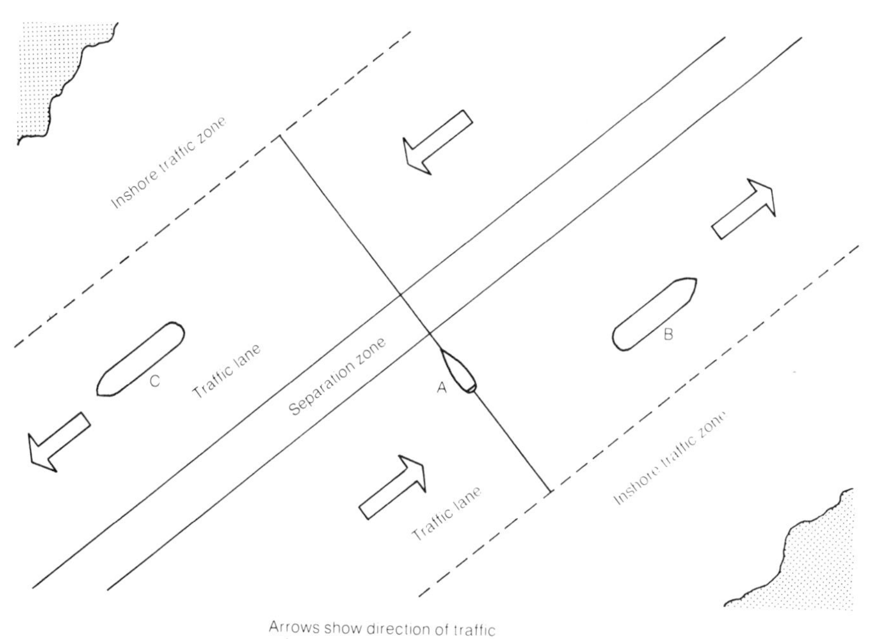


**Fig. 14.4** Crossing shipping lanes. Boat A must cross as quickly as possible at right angles to the traffic using the traffic lanes (boats B and C).

There are also inshore traffic zones which may be used by small craft.

Illustrated in the following figures are: rules for sailing boats (Fig. 14.5), rules for boats under power (Fig. 14.6), the overtaking rule (Fig. 14.7), lights, shapes and fog signals (Figs 14.8 to 14.10), and rules for smaller boats (Fig. 14.11).

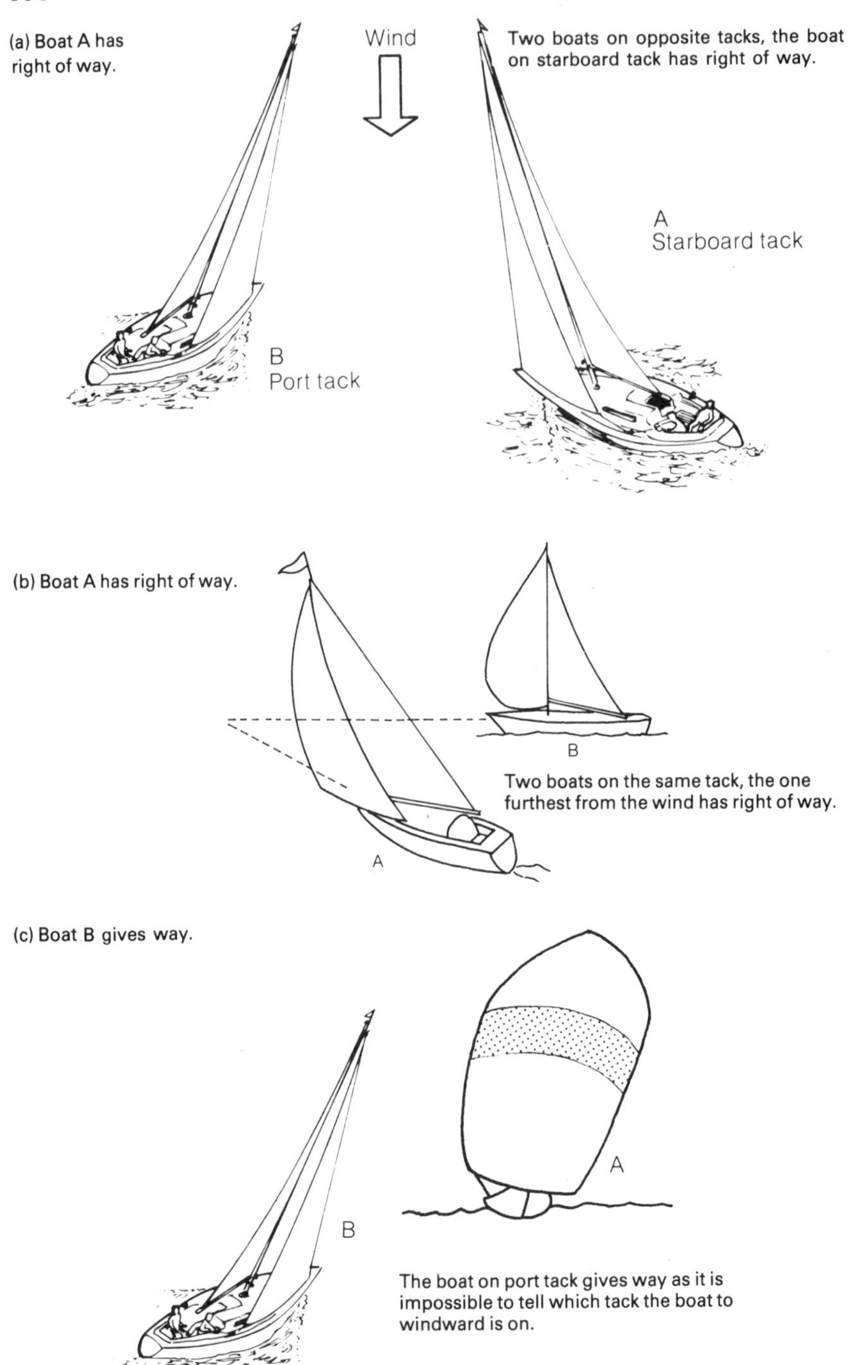


**Fig. 14.5** Rules for sailing boats.

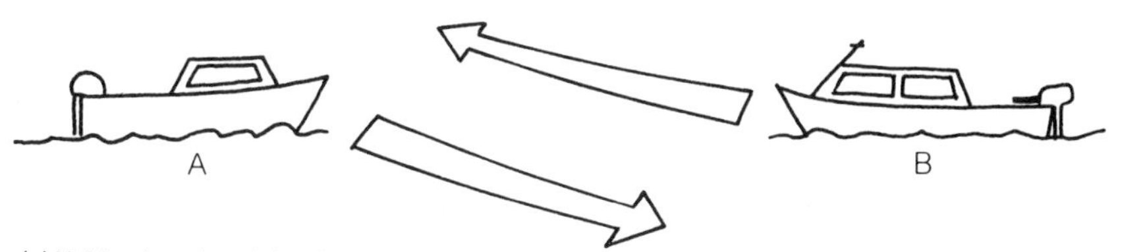


(a) Neither boat has right of way. Two power boats on reciprocal courses, both alter course to starboard.

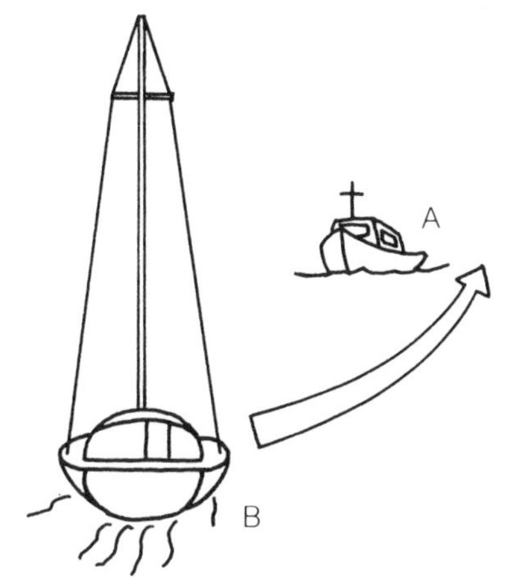


(b) Boat A has right of way. Two boats under power, the one which has the other on her starboard side keeps clear.

**Fig. 14.6** Rules for boats under power.

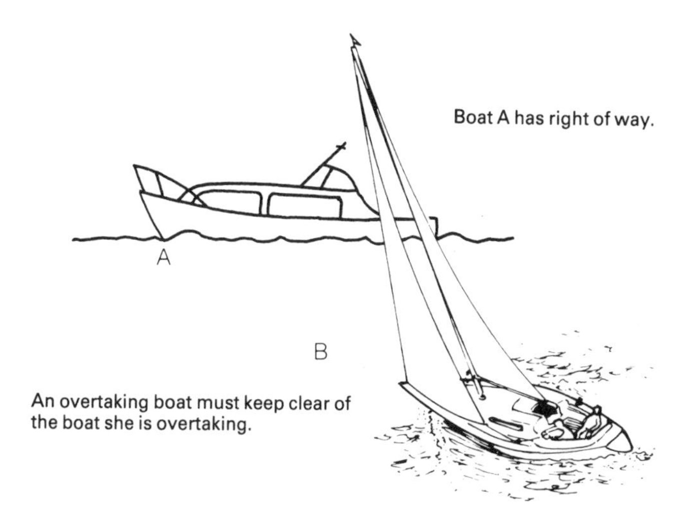


**Fig. 14.7** Overtaking boat.

## Lights, shapes and fog signals

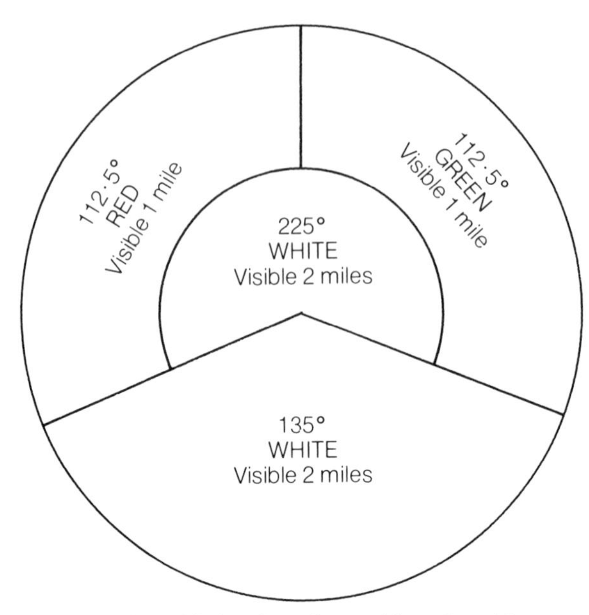


**Fig. 14.8** Arc and visibility of lights for a boat of less than 12 metres in length.

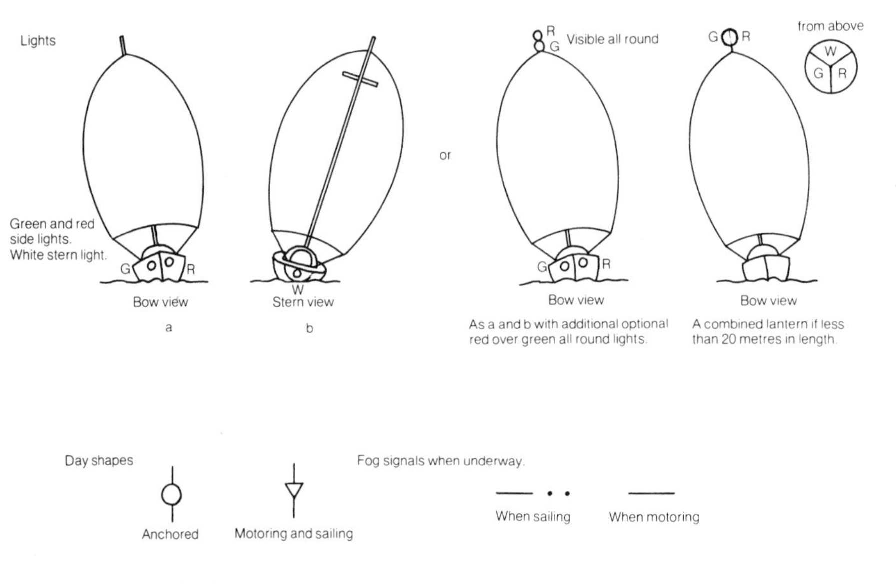


**Fig. 14.9** A sailing boat.

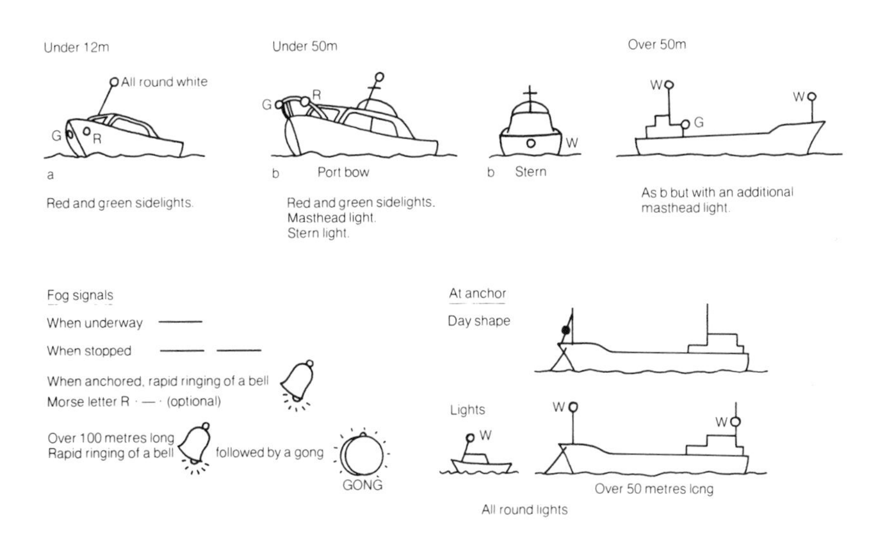


**Fig. 14.10** A power driven boat.

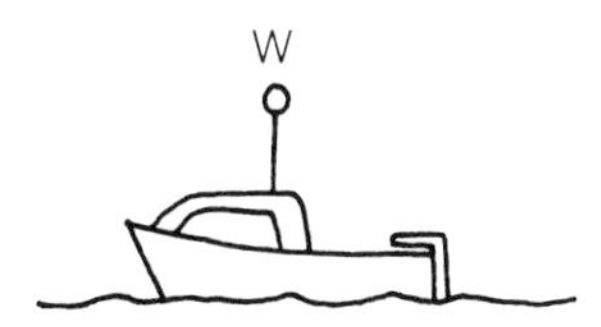


A boat under power of less than seven metres may show just an all round white light if it is not practicable to show side lights.

A sailing boat of less than seven metres or a boat being rowed should have a torch ready to exhibit when required.

**Fig. 14.11** Smaller boats.

*Signals used when vessels are in sight of one another*

|  |  |  |
| --- | --- | --- |
| ● | One short blast | I am altering course to starboard. |
| ●● | Two short blasts | I am altering course to port |
| ●●● | Three short blasts | My engines are going astern. |
| ●●●●● | Five short blasts | I am unsure of your intentions. |
| ●●●● ● | Four short blasts followed by one short blast | I intend to turn completely around to starboard. |
| ●●●● ●● | Four short blasts followed by two short blasts | I intend to turn completely around to port. |
| ▬ ▬ ● | Two long blasts followed by one short blast | I wish to overtake you on your starboard side. |
| ▬ ▬ ●● | Two long blasts followed by two short blasts | I wish to overtake you on your port side. |
| ▬ ● ▬ ● | One long blast, one short blast, one long blast, one short blast | You may overtake me on the side indicated. |

*Chapter Fifteen*

# Courtesy Costs Nothing

It is always a pleasure to be a member of the crew of a smart boat. Much of this smart impression is created by smooth execution of manoeuvres, but also important is observance of the rules of etiquette and courtesy.

## Flag etiquette

A cruising boat is properly dressed flying a masthead burgee and her national ensign.

### THE BURGEE

The burgee is usually that of a club or association of which the skipper is a member, and is flown at all times when the boat is in commission with the skipper on board or absent for a period of no longer than 24 hours.

### THE ENSIGN

The ensign is normally red. Other ensigns (blue or white) can be worn only if authorised by special warrant. At sea, the ensign is worn at all times. In harbour it is hoisted at 0800 in summer and 0900 in winter time and is lowered at sunset or 2000 whichever is earlier. When passing a warship of any nationality it is courteous to dip the ensign by lowering it until the warship responds by dipping and hoisting hers. The ensign is not worn when racing.

### THE COURTESY ENSIGN

When visiting a foreign country the ensign of that country should be flown from the starboard spreader from arrival in, to departure from, the territorial waters. This is known as a courtesy ensign.

### HOUSE FLAG

This is a rectangular flag with a design personal to the owner. The house flag is flown from the starboard spreader under the same circumstances as the burgee. If a courtesy ensign is flown from the starboard spreader, then the house flag is flown on the port spreader.

### INTERNATIONAL CODE FLAGS

These may be flown to indicate their code meanings on the starboard spreader or, if this is already occupied, from the port spreader. More common flags are:

| | *Description* | | *Meaning* |
|---|---|---|---|
| Flag Q | *shape*:<br>*colour*: | rectangular<br>yellow | Boat requesting customs clearance |
| Flag A | *shape*:<br>*colour*: | swallow tail<br>blue and white | Diver operating |
| Flag B | *shape*:<br>*colour*: | swallow tail<br>red | Carrying, loading or unloading a dangerous cargo |
| Flag R over Flag Y | *shape*:<br>*colour* R:<br><br>*colour* Y: | rectangular (both)<br>yellow cross on a red ground<br>red and yellow diagonal stripes | Keep well clear and go at slow speed when passing me |
| Flag N over Flag C | *shape*:<br>N *colour*:<br>C *colour*: | rectangular (both)<br>blue and white chequered<br>red horizontal band with a white horizontal band each side on a blue ground | International distress signal |

### DRESSING A SHIP OVERALL

For special occasions when in harbour international code flags are hoisted from the stem to the masthead(s) and back to the stern. She is then dressed overall.

## Behaviour in port

When berthing alongside another boat, if anyone is on board it is normal to ask if you may come alongside. You should provide your own fenders and not rely upon the other boat to do so.

If other boats have to be crossed to get ashore this should be done by passing over their foredeck and not across the cockpit making as little noise as possible especially late at night. On first crossing such a boat, ask permission to do so. Try to tread as lightly as possible, and do not put weight or pressure on fittings which look inadequate.

*Chapter Sixteen*

# Engines

## Diesel engines

Most small boat inboard engines are diesels. They do not have ignition and sparking plugs like petrol engines and can thus run without a battery. They usually incorporate a flywheel which has to be rotated rapidly (either by hand or with an electric motor) to start. For cold starting there is either a decompression lever, which is up or off until the flywheel is rotating fast enough and then pushed down; or a pre-heater which is switched on for about 20 seconds before rotating the flywheel.

Once a diesel is running, it likes to keep running fairly fast and under load. It will give full power as soon as it is started without warming up. When starting from cold, it should not be run for short intervals and then stopped.

To stop a diesel there is usually a special spring-operated stop lever, or sometimes an electrically operated switch.

The main problem with a diesel is fuel contamination, so the first check is to clear any water or dirt accumulated in the fuel. Most water comes from condensation in fuel tanks left nearly empty in cold weather. If water does get into the fuel it is normally trapped in a water separator which can be cleared of water and dirt by opening its drain plug. If water gets beyond the water separator then it has to be removed by bleeding the fuel system – not a difficult job in harbour but quite tricky at sea.

## Petrol engines

These have similar problems to cars. Sparking plugs must be kept clean and dry and the gaps correctly set. Petrol is a volatile liquid with a lower flash point than diesel and so any leaks are more dangerous and constitute a fire risk.

## Daily checks

All engines react badly to sea water so they must be kept clean and dry. If an engine has been immersed in salt water it must be washed thoroughly with fresh water and dried out as soon as possible.

### INBOARD ENGINE

Check the oil level in the engine and the gear box.
Check for oil and fuel leaks.
Check for water in the fuel.
See that the batteries are charged.
Check the fuel level.
Check that the cooling water seacock is open if the engine is going to be used.
If cooled by sea water check that it is circulating properly.
If cooled by fresh water see that the water tank is full.

### OUTBOARD ENGINE

See that the fuel tank is full and also the spare fuel can.
Check that the sparking plugs are clean and the gaps correctly set.
Carry spare sparking plugs and a plug spanner.
Keep the bearings greased.
See that the correct oil/petrol mixture is used.
When running check that the cooling water is circulating by watching the outlet.
When it has finished running, run fresh water through the cooling system if possible then thoroughly dry the outside of the engine.

*Chapter Seventeen*

# Emergencies

## Man overboard

It is important that each member of the crew can take the helm and get the boat back to a person who has fallen overboard. The method used to bring the boat back alongside the person will depend upon: (1) The experience of the helmsman; (2) The weather conditions; (3) The visibility; (4) The type of boat. It may well be that a novice can only do this manoeuvre under power so, if the engine is serviceable, there is no reason why it should not be used. However, in case of engine failure it is necessary to know and practise at least one method of bringing the boat back under sail and the good skipper will train his crew accordingly, practising with a fender or other floating object. Do not ever practise man overboard drill by asking a member of the crew to jump into the water.

Four methods are described below. Whichever is used, the objective is to get back to the person quickly and stop the boat alongside him. In cold water, survival time is counted in minutes not hours. The following routine applies to all methods:

1. Immediately someone falls overboard shout 'man overboard' to alert all the crew.
2. Throw the lifebuoy (and the dan buoy, if carried) into the water, activating the light if at night.
3. Point continuously towards the person in the water calling out his relative position and distance off. Do not take your eyes off him. In a rough sea or at night he can be lost to view very quickly.
4. It is a good idea to throw in other floating objects periodically so that a trail is left which can be followed when the boat turns round and heads back.
5. If a spinnaker is set, course should be altered towards the wind and the spinnaker lowered behind the mainsail, stowing it in the

cabin out of the way. Similarly, if the engine is to be used, the mainsail should be lowered.

6. Make a check to see that no lines are trailing over the side which could get around the propeller.
7. Make a note of the time, the course and log reading in case the person is lost to sight and it is necessary to retrace the boat's track.

METHOD 1; SAILING

Whatever point of sailing the boat is on, she immediately goes on to a reach and sails a sufficient distance away (5 to 7 boat lengths) from the man in the water to enable the boat to reverse course and return under full control. When the boat is ready she tacks round on to the opposite reach and sails back along her previous track. The final approach is made on a fine reach with both sails flying so that the boat can be stopped with the person to leeward ready for the pick up.

Using this method the boat is fully under control and the crew can sort themselves out, but it does require a certain amount of sailing skill and also takes the boat a distance away from the person in the water.

METHOD 2; SAILING

In a light wind the boat may be gybed round. However, if the winds are strong or the helmsman inexperienced, damage to the boat and possibly a further accident may occur. When running in light airs or if just a headsail is set, this method is preferable. It does require the helmsman to have a good knowledge of the boat's handling capabilities.

METHOD 3; SAILING BOAT UNDER POWER

Immediately heave-to and start the engine. Lower the sails and secure or, if shorthanded, drop the mainsail and let the headsail fly. Make sure no sheets are trailing in the water. This method is within the capabilities of an inexperienced crew provided he has been shown how to heave-to. When the person in the water has been reached and secured, the engine must be stopped to avoid possible injury from the propeller.

METHOD 4; POWER BOAT

Steer the propeller away from the person in the water by altering course towards the side over which he has fallen. Turn a tight circle to come up alongside, with the boat head to wind.

### THE PICK-UP

It is extremely difficult to lift a waterlogged person out of the water, especially if he is unconscious. Whilst the boat is returning to the man in the water a line should be prepared with a bowline in the end. The free end is secured to the boat and the loop can either be placed over the man's head to fit around his waist or he can put his foot into it and use it as a ladder. If a boarding ladder is available this should indeed be used. A lifebelt (or quoit) with a light floating line attached should be available to throw to the person if the helmsman misjudges the final approach.

If the man is unconscious it may be necessary for another crew member to go into the water to secure a rope around him. If this is necessary that person must be wearing a lifejacket and must have a separate lifeline attached to the boat.

*Lifting out*
To lift the man out of the water one of the sail halyards can be attached to him and the winch used: or the luff of a small sail (such as the storm jib) can be clipped on to the guardrail with the bight of the sail lowered into the water and floated under him. The halyard is then attached to the clew of the sail and he is winched out of the water. If it can be done quickly it may be worth inflating the dinghy and getting him into that first.

## The liferaft

Everyone on board should know how to inflate and board the liferaft.

### LAUNCHING

Do not launch the liferaft until the last minute as it may capsize in rough weather. Do not leave the boat if it is still afloat: abandoned boats have been found still floating with no survivors.

1. Make sure that the liferaft's painter is secured to a strong point on the boat before it is launched.
2. Release the fastening which secures the raft to the boat and launch it.
3. When it is in the water take up the slack on the painter and then tug sharply: this should inflate the raft.

BOARDING

1. Do not jump into the raft.
2. Get the heaviest person in first to stabilise it.
3. When everyone is aboard, cut the painter and paddle away from the boat.
4. Stream the drogue.
5. Elect a leader.
6. Take seasickness tablets.
7. Check for leaks.
8. Locate first aid kit, flares, repair kit, survival kit.
9. Do not issue drinking water for 24 hours unless anyone is injured and bleeding.
10. Do not drink sea water or urine.
11. Keep warm.
12. Keep a lookout and try to estimate your position.

## Collision

In many emergencies it is difficult to establish a correct priority. Traditionally, the safety of the boat comes first and the safety of the crew next. If a boat has been in a collision, the first priority is normally to control the flooding. Once it has been established that the boat itself is in no further danger of sinking or catching fire, then any injuries to the crew can be treated.

To stop a flood, push blankets or sleeping bags into the hole from the inside and, if possible, drape a sail over the hole from outside. It has been said that a frightened man with a bucket is the best way of emptying a boat full of water. However, the main bilge pump with high capacity should be used. The toilet pump may also be used, particularly if a length of tubing from the bilges is fed into the pan of the toilet. The hose from the engine cooling water system could possibly be disconnected and placed in the bilges. When the engine is run water will be sucked up through it and discharged overboard.

## Fire

A fire on a boat at sea can be very alarming. If the fire looks as though it might get out of hand, prepare to abandon ship. Get the dinghy inflated and tow it astern. See that the liferaft is ready to launch immediately. Don lifejackets and then standby to initiate distress procedures.

The best way to deal with a fire is to smother it (thus starving it of oxygen) and to prevent it spreading by keeping the surrounding areas cool.

The most common source of fire is the cooker. This should never be left unattended. If a frying pan has caught alight the flames should be smothered with the fire blanket (or a damp blanket) by placing it away from yourself over the flames. Do not attempt to throw a blazing frying pan overboard as it is likely to set the rest of the boat alight.

Water should not be thrown on oil fires as this spreads the fire. Smothering it with sand or using a dry powder or BCF (bromo-chloro-difluoro-methane) extinguisher is effective although the latter gives off toxic fumes and should not be used in a confined space.

Fires down below may be caused by people smoking. Smoking should be confined to the upper deck. A sleeping bag which catches fire can be doused with water.

Once a fire has occurred, although it may appear to be extinguished it should be watched in case it relights. Bilges should be kept clean and well ventilated so that gas and fuel fumes do not accumulate.

Gas bottles should be outside in the cockpit where any leaks will drain overboard and not into the bilges. They should be turned off at the bottle when not in use. The gas in the pipes can be burned out by turning the gas off at the bottle before turning it off at the cooker.

The engine should be checked regularly for fuel and oil leaks. Hatches should be closed when refuelling and if any fuel spillage occurs, the boat should be hosed down and ventilated.

## Accidents

The skipper should ascertain before leaving harbour if anyone is likely to require special medical attention or is taking medication. Every crew member should be able to cope with minor ailments and, in the event of a major accident, be able to make the patient as comfortable as possible so that injuries may be contained until help arrives.

### MINOR ACCIDENTS

*Small cuts*

Wash and cleanse with disinfectant and cover with a plaster or dressing.

*Burns and scalds*

Immediately flood the area with cold water for at least 10 minutes and then cover with a smooth clean dry cloth.

*Bruises*
Apply a cold compress.

*Seasickness*
Give the patient something to do which requires concentration. If severe send him below and tell him to lie down.

*Headache*
Give aspirin or some other type of tablet recommended for headache.

*Sunburn*
Cool with calomine lotion and cover to prevent further burning.

*Strains and sprains*
Rest the affected limb.

## MAJOR ACCIDENTS

*Severe bleeding*
Pinch the flesh together, raise the limb or press pads of material on to the wound.

*Internal bleeding*
Lie the patient down, keep warm and try to get help.

*Dislocations and fractures*
Immobilise the limb in the most comfortable position until help arrives.

## SHOCK

This accompanies all injuries.

*Symptoms*
The patient appears pale, his skin feels clammy, he may be perspiring, vomiting, thirsty or over-anxious. His pulse may be weak.

*Treatment*
Treat by lying down with the head low and turned to one side. Loosen the clothing. Keep warm by covering with a sail, blanket or sleeping bag. Reassure him. If the underlying injury is not apparent try to find and treat it.

CONCUSSION/COMPRESSION

Any head injuries can become serious. After any bleeding has been dealt with the patient should be watched for drowsiness, dilated pupils, garbled speech and bleeding from the ears or nose (especially if he has been unconscious). Fluid in the brain cavity or a depressed bone may be compressing the brain and the patient can go into a coma. These cases should always be referred to a doctor as soon as possible.

COMA POSITION

Any patient liable to vomit should be placed into the position shown in Fig. 17.1 so that he does not choke (provided that there is no injury to prevent this).

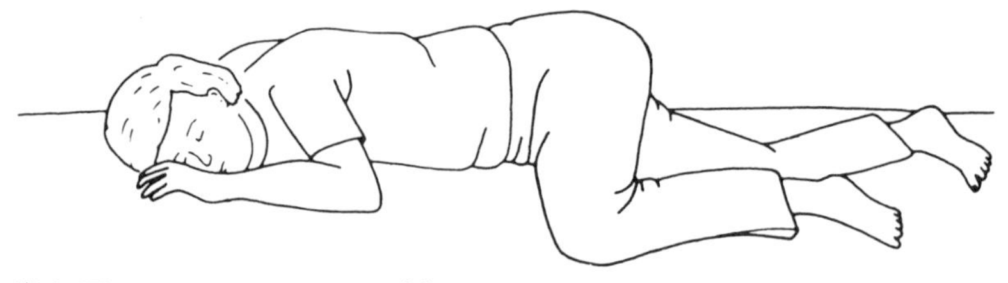

**Fig. 17.1** The recovery or coma position.

HYPOTHERMIA

Anyone who is rescued from cold water when the inner core of the body has been cooled, should be treated for hypothermia. If this is not done he could quickly die.

*Symptoms*
Collapse, feeling cold, shivering, cramp, irritability, unnatural quietness, lack of co-ordination, loss of energy, forgetfulness, pallor and cold to the touch.

*Treatment*
Prevent further heat loss by protecting him from the wind and weather. Get him below and wrap him in a sleeping bag or several blankets. If an exposure blanket (a plastic sheet with a reflective surface) or a large plastic bag is available, this can be put round him to contain body heat. Unless medical advice is available re-warming should be slow without the use of hot water bottles. *No alcohol must be given.* Placing near a warm engine will help.

When lifted out of the water he should be treated with care and kept in a horizontal position.

RESUSCITATION

When breathing has stopped it is necessary to start resuscitation. Unless this is done within four minutes brain damage may occur.

*Expired air resuscitation*

1. Lie the patient on his back.
2. Clear his mouth of obstructions and check whether he has swallowed his tongue (but do not waste time).
3. Tilt his head back and lift his jaw as shown in Fig. 17.2. This lifts the tongue away from the back of the throat and creates an open airway.
4. Pinch his nose and blow firmly into his mouth or close his mouth with your thumb and blow gently but firmly into his nose. Whichever method is used see that a good seal is made. His chest should rise, if it does not, check for obstructions.
5. Turn your head away, wait for his chest to fall, take a breath and repeat. Initially give 4 to 6 quick breaths and then one every 5 seconds.
6. Continue until he is breathing normally or until there is no hope of recovery.
7. If normal breathing is resumed watch him carefully to see that his breathing does not fail again.

For small children and babies more rapid breathing is needed. Be careful not to blow too hard as the lungs may be damaged. If a person's heart has stopped beating closed chest cardiac massage

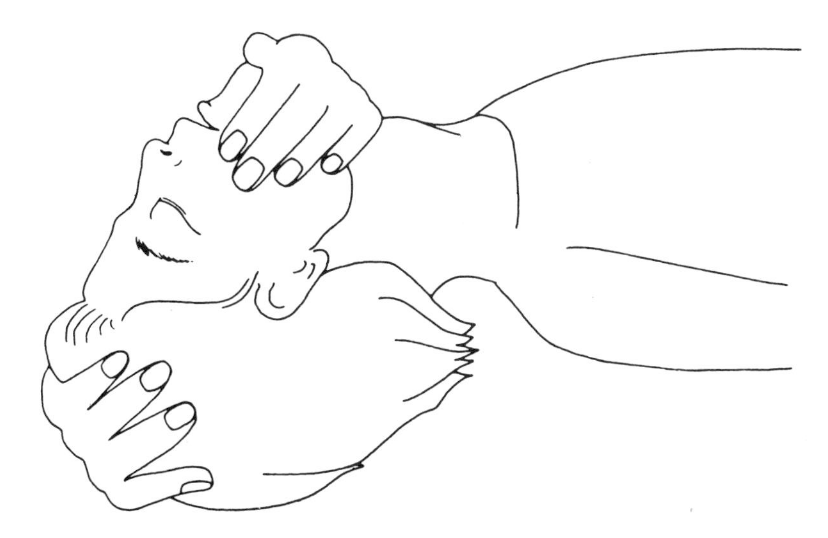

**Fig. 17.2** The correct position of the head for mouth-to-mouth resuscitation.

should be applied. This needs to have been properly learned, however, if it is to be successful.

Any person who has suffered a hit on the head and become unconscious, had severe hypothermia, or recovered from an apparent drowning should be referred to a doctor as soon as possible.

## Contents of a first aid kit

The first aid kit should be kept in a watertight box and a list of the contents should be on the outside of the box. The following is a basic kit:

Roll of plaster
Individual plasters
Large triangular bandages
Small bandages
Lint
Cotton wool
Scissors
Tweezers
Eye lotion and eye bath
Calomine lotion
Safety pins
Disinfectant
Aspirin
Seasickness tablets
Indigestion tablets
Exposure bag
First aid book

First aid has been dealt with here only briefly. During the winter months it is a good idea to attend a first aid course and learn how to administer it thoroughly.

## Distress

All crew members must know the distress procedures and should acquaint themselves with the operation of flares and signalling lamp (if available). A distress signal is only used when there is grave and imminent danger to the boat. The distress signals are listed fully in Annexe IV of the International Regulations for Preventing Collisions at Sea.

Those suitable for a small boat are:

1. Continuous sounding of the fog horn.
2. The morse letters S O S by light or sound.
3. The word MAYDAY on the radio telephone.
4. International Code Flags N over C.
5. A square shape above or below a round shape.
6. A red rocket parachute flare or red hand flare.
7. An orange smoke signal by day.
8. Outstretched arms slowly and repeatedly raised and lowered.
9. Flames on the boat.

10. An explosive device (such as a gun) fired at intervals of one minute.

## PYROTECHNICS

*Red flares*
A red hand flare (pinpoint flare) is for use when within sight of land or another boat, or to pinpoint your position when the rescue services are approaching. Do not point it into the wind or you will be covered with sparks and smoke. Do not look directly at it. A red parachute rocket flare is for use when out of sight of land. Rockets turn towards the wind and so should be fired vertically, or in strong winds 15 degrees downwind. If there is low cloud it should be fired 45 degrees downwind so that it ignites below the cloud base.

*White hand flare*
This is not a distress signal but is used to warn other boats of your position. It is very bright so you should not look directly at it.

*Orange smoke signal*
This is a daytime distress signal which produces a dense cloud of orange smoke that is easily seen from the air. In a strong wind, however, the smoke blows along the sea surface and may not be visible from the shore or from other boats.

## VHF RADIO TELEPHONE EMERGENCY PROCEDURE

The VHF (very high frequency) radio telephone is similar to a normal telephone. It usually has a switch which is depressed when speaking and released when listening. It is the quickest way to summon help. Its range is about 30 miles, dependent upon the height of the aerial.

*Sending a distress (MAYDAY) call*
This is used when the vessel is in grave and imminent danger.

1. Switch on the set and select Channel 16.
2. Listen to ensure that no other station is transmitting.
3. Depress the press-to-speak switch and say MAYDAY three times.
4. Say the words THIS IS and the BOAT'S NAME three times.
5. Repeat MAYDAY and the BOAT'S NAME once.
6. Give the boat's position either as latitude and longitude, or as a bearing *from* and distance off a known geographical point.
7. Give the nature of the distress and the assistance required.

8. Give the number of people on board.
9. End the message with the word OVER.

Release the press-to-speak switch and wait. Repeat if there is no reply within 3 minutes.

*Example 3*

MAYDAY MAYDAY MAYDAY
THIS IS YACHT JETTO YACHT JETTO YACHT JETTO
MAYDAY YACHT JETTO
MY POSITION IS ONE FIVE ZERO BEACHY HEAD LIGHT ONE POINT FIVE MILES
I AM SINKING AND NEED IMMEDIATE ASSISTANCE
I HAVE FOUR PERSONS ON BOARD
OVER

*Sending an URGENCY (PAN PAN) call*

This is used for a very urgent message concerning the safety of a person or the safety of the vessel. It is not yet a distress situation but may become so.

1. Switch on the set and select Channel 16.
2. Listen to ensure that no other station is transmitting.
3. Depress the press-to-speak switch and say PAN PAN three times.
4. Call anyone listening by using the words ALL STATIONS three times.
5. Give the BOAT'S NAME three times.
6. Give the boat's position.
7. Give the reason for the call and the help needed.
8. End the message with the word OVER.

Release the press-to-speak switch and wait for a reply.

*Example 4*

PAN PAN PAN PAN PAN PAN
ALL STATIONS ALL STATIONS ALL STATIONS
THIS IS YACHT JETTO YACHT JETTO YACHT JETTO
MY POSITION IS TWO SEVEN ZERO FROM NEEDLES LIGHTHOUSE SIX MILES
MY ENGINE HAS FAILED I AM DRIFTING AND NEED A TOW URGENTLY
OVER

MEDICAL ASSISTANCE

It may be that you have a sick crew member and are not sure of the diagnosis. Medical advice can be obtained using the VHF radio telephone by including the word MEDICO after the words PAN PAN. The call is sent exactly the same as for a normal urgency call but is usually addressed to the nearest Coast Radio Station instead of to all stations. After initial contact has been made on Channel 16 you may be asked to change to a less busy working channel if there is to be a lengthy conversation with a doctor.

# Question Papers

# QUESTION PAPER ONE

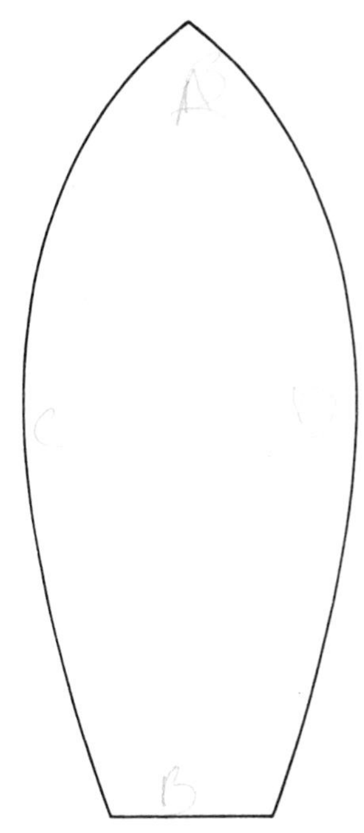

**1.1** Fill in on the diagram:
a. bow b. stern c. port side d. starboard side.

**1.2** Study the diagram and answer the following questions.
In relation to the boat, where are:
a. The buoy b. The rowing boat c. The power boat.

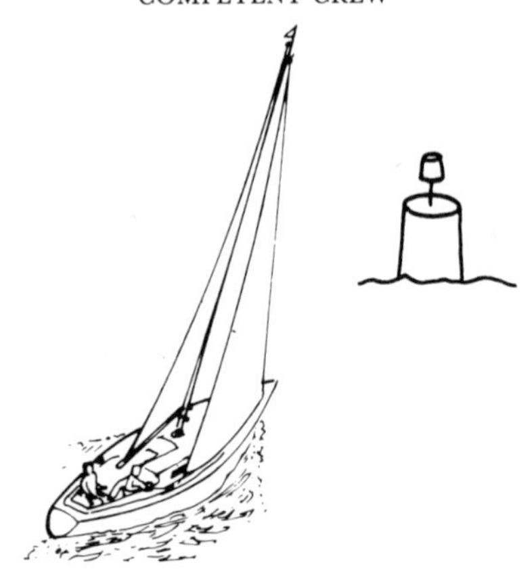

**1.3** In the diagram the boat is approaching a buoy. How would you tell the skipper that you wish him to pass the buoy so that it is on the port side of the boat?

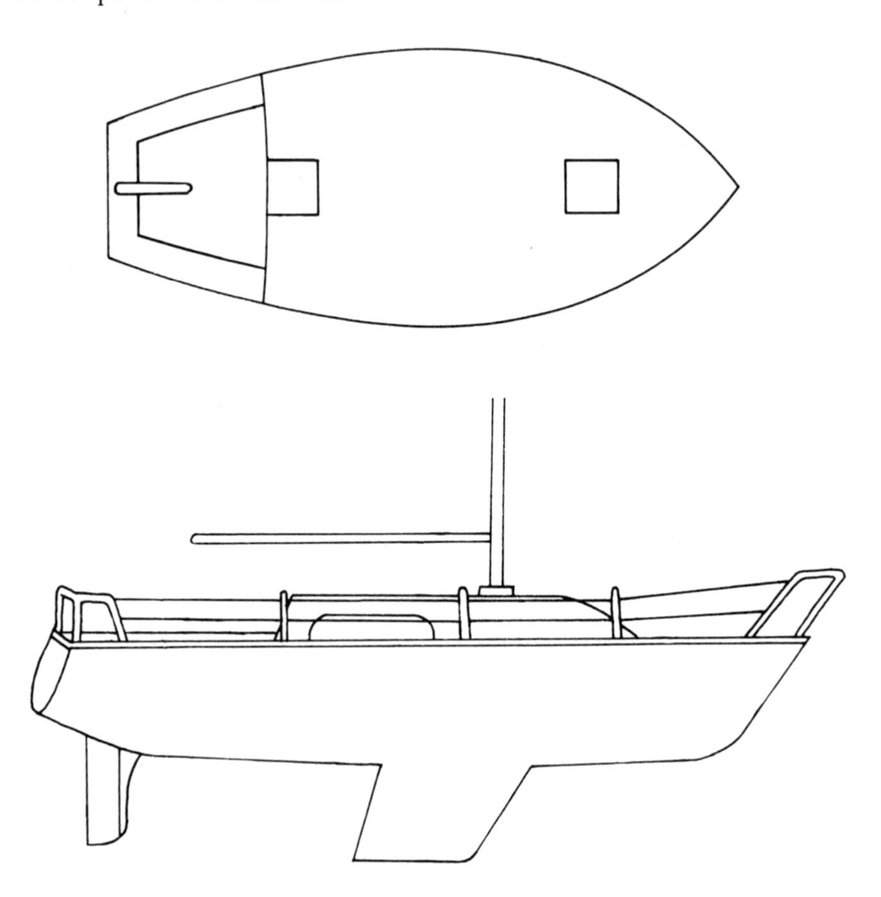

**1.4** Fill in the following names on the diagram (below, left):

| | | | | | |
|---|---|---|---|---|---|
| a. | Fore hatch | b. | Main hatch | c. | Cockpit |
| d. | Mast | e. | Boom | f. | Pulpit |
| g. | Pushpit | h. | Guardrail | i. | Stanchion |
| j. | Keel | k. | Rudder | l. | Tiller |

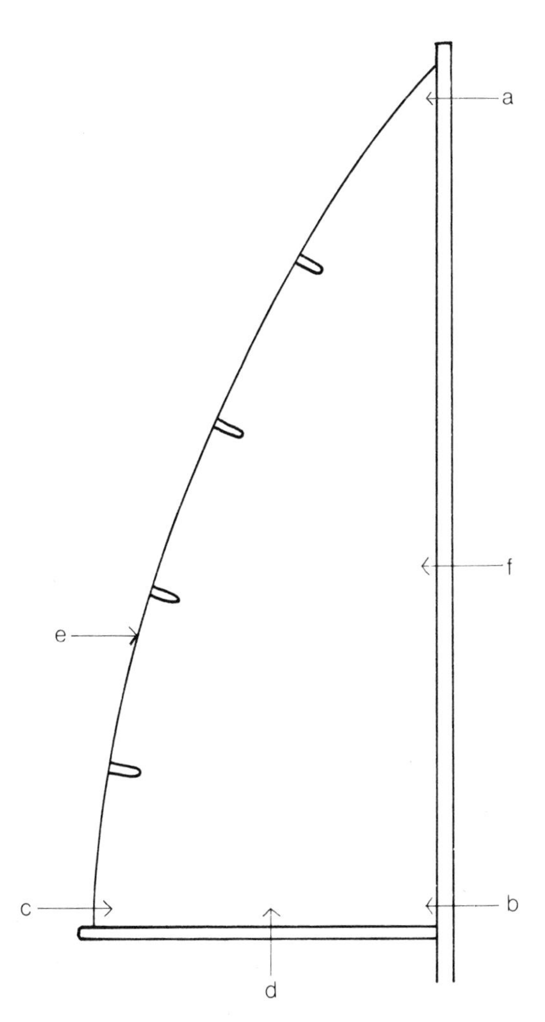


**1.5** Name the parts of the sail

# QUESTION PAPER TWO

**2.1** Fill in the points of sailing.

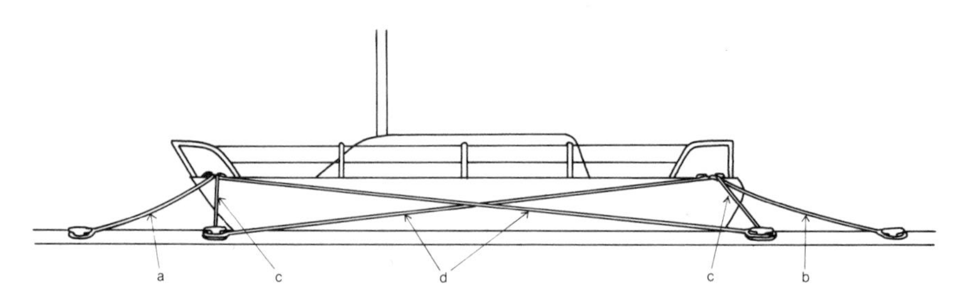


**2.2** I What are the lines a, b, c and d called?
II What is their purpose?

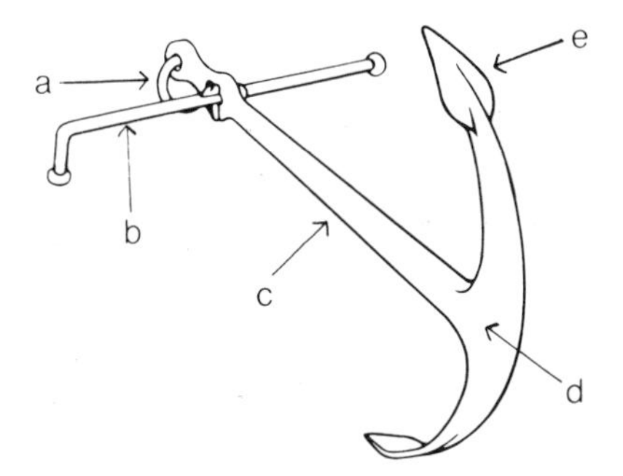


**2.3** What are the parts of the anchor called?

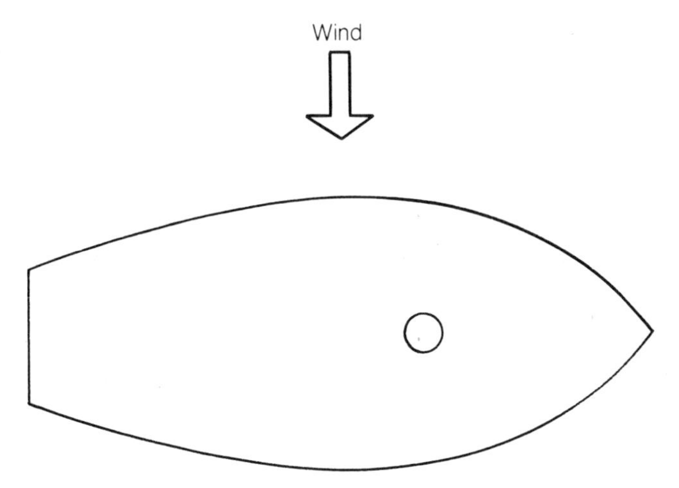


**2.4** Show the position of the sails and the rudder when the boat is hove-to.

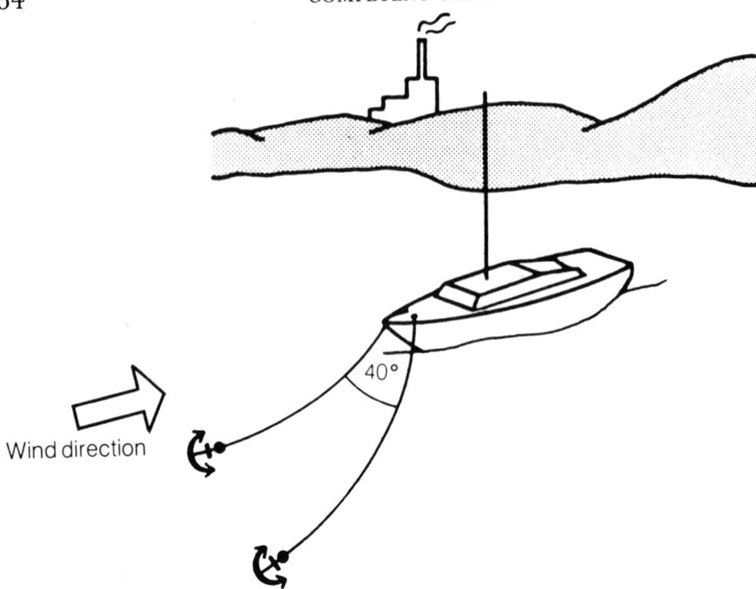


**2.5** Why has the boat in the diagram laid a second anchor? The tidal stream is weak in the anchorage but a gale has been forecast.

# QUESTION PAPER THREE

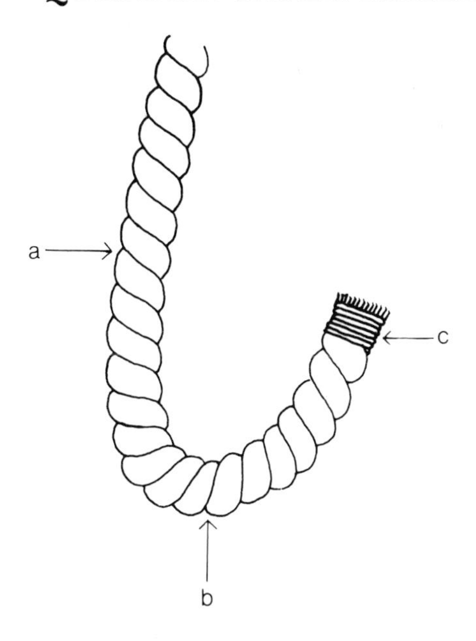


**3.1** What are the parts of the rope called?

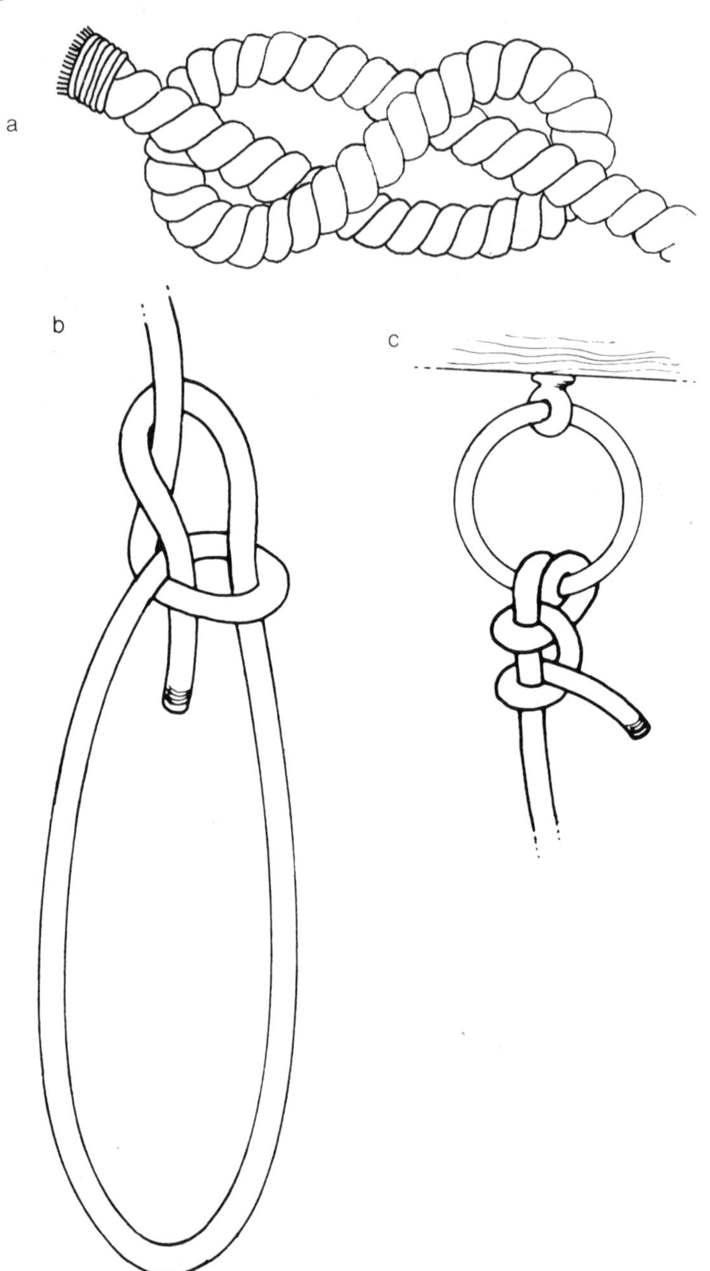


**3.2** I What are these knots or hitches called?
II What are they used for?

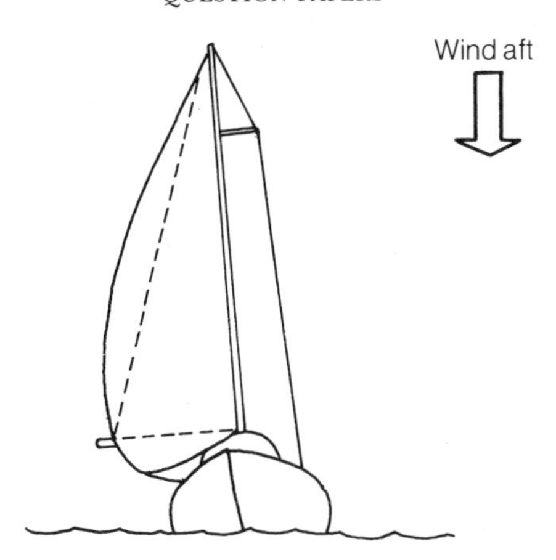


**3.3** The boat in the diagram is carrying a full mainsail and a large genoa. A gale has been forecast. If she stays on the same course and the wind increases to force 8, what sails would you expect her to carry?

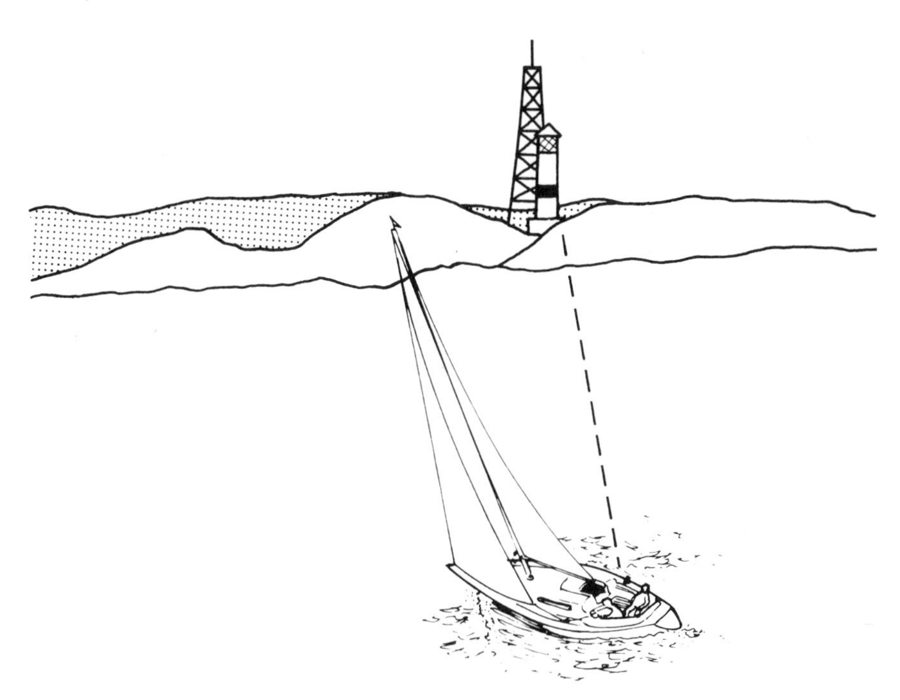

**3.4** The boat in the diagram takes a compass bearing of the lighthouse and the radio mast when they are in transit which gives 356° C. The true bearing on the chart is 358° T. Variation is 6° W. What is the deviation?

**3.5** The diagram shows a hand bearing compass being used to take a bearing. What corrections should be made to that bearing before it can be plotted on the chart?

# QUESTION PAPER FOUR

**4.1** Draw arrows to show the conventional direction of buoyage around the British Isles.

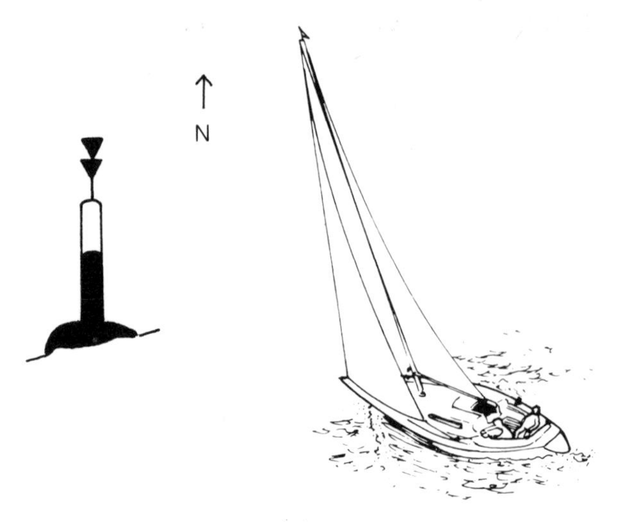


**4.2** The boat is approaching a cardinal mark. Which side should she leave it?

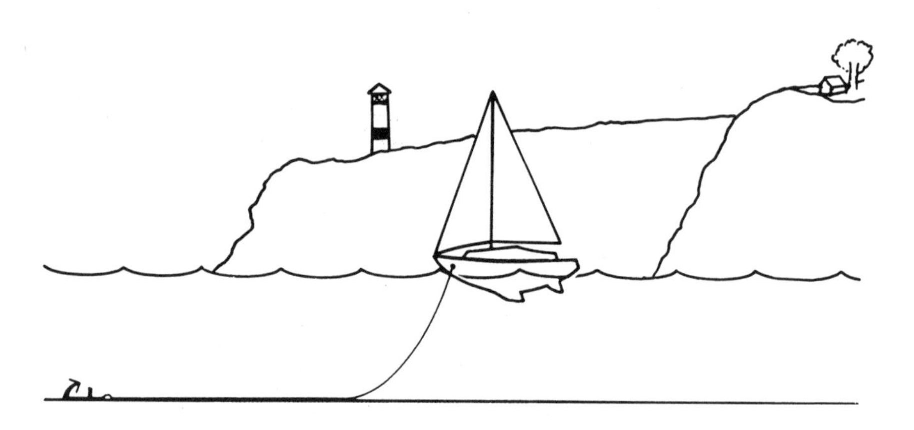

**4.3** The boat in the diagram has just anchored. How can she tell whether her anchor is dragging?

**4.4** How can the boat use shore objects to enter the harbour safely?

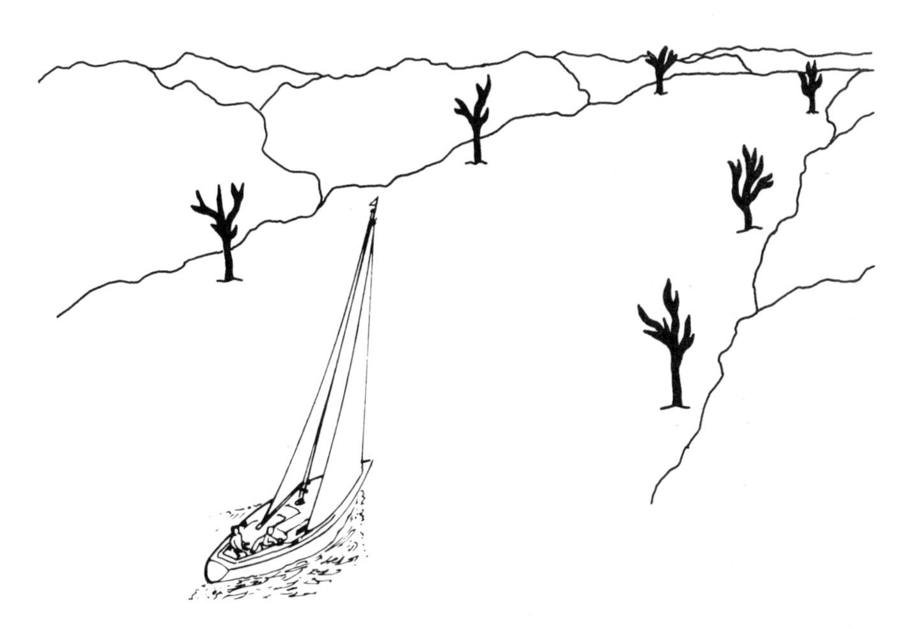

**4.5** I What are the tree branches stuck in the mud called?
II What are they for?

# QUESTION PAPER FIVE

**5.1** How can the power boat tell whether she is on a collision course with the sailing boat?

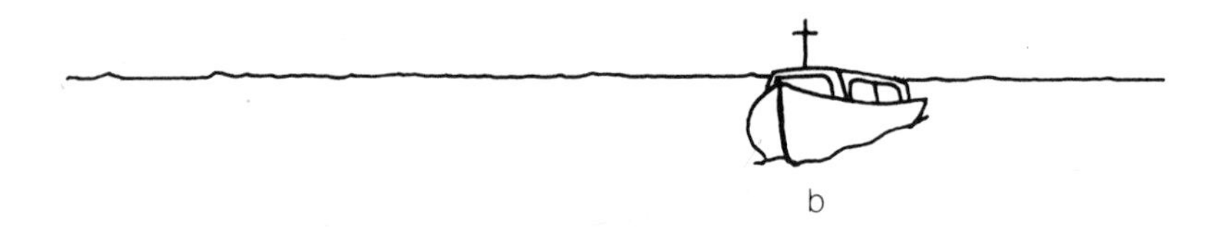


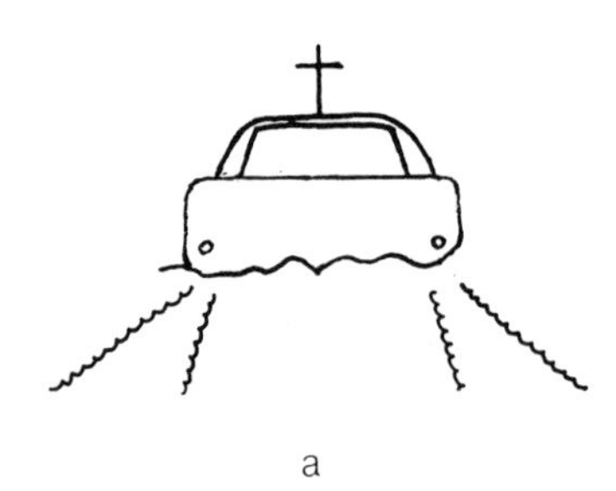


**5.2** Who has right of way?

**5.3** The sailing boat is overtaking the power boat. Who has right of way?

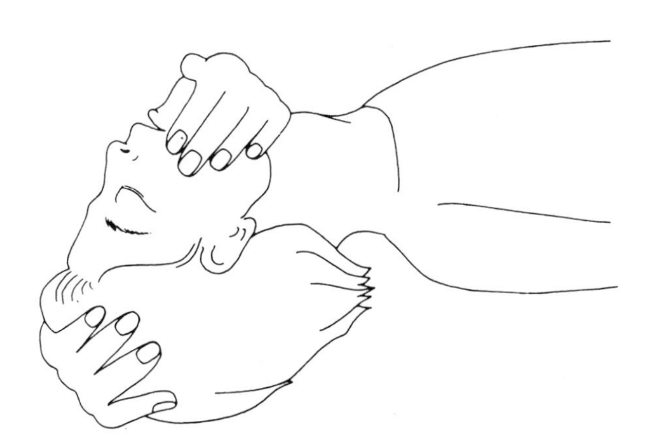

**5.4** Why is the patient's head placed in the above position before commencing expired air resuscitation?

**5.5** Yacht Mermain is holed and sinking rapidly. Her position is five miles from Land's End. The bearing of Land's End from the yacht is 060° T. There are six people on board. Write out the message she will send on the VHF radio telephone.

# Answers to Question Papers

## ONE

**1.1**

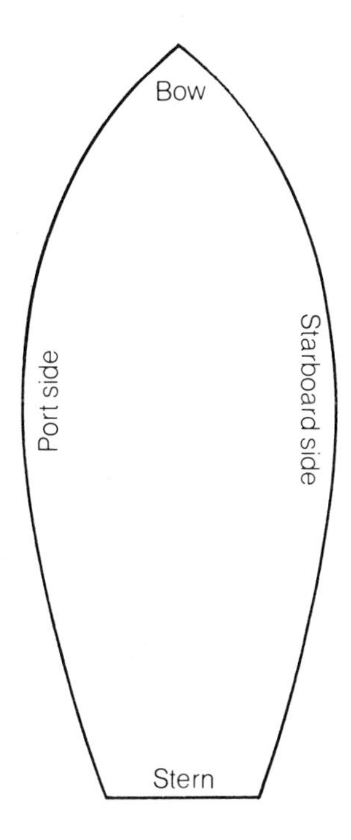


**1.2** a. Astern b. Abeam to port. c. Ahead.

**1.3** Leave the buoy to port.

**1.4**

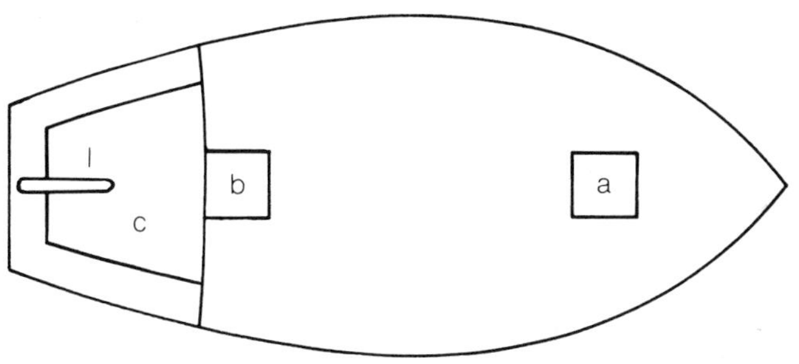


*continued*

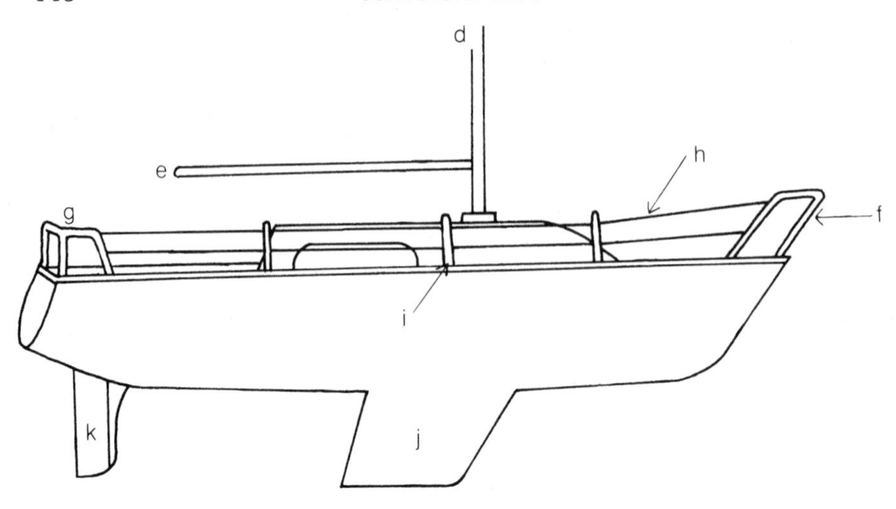


**1.5** a. Head b. Tack. c. Clew. d. Foot. e. Leech. f. Luff.

## TWO

**2.1**

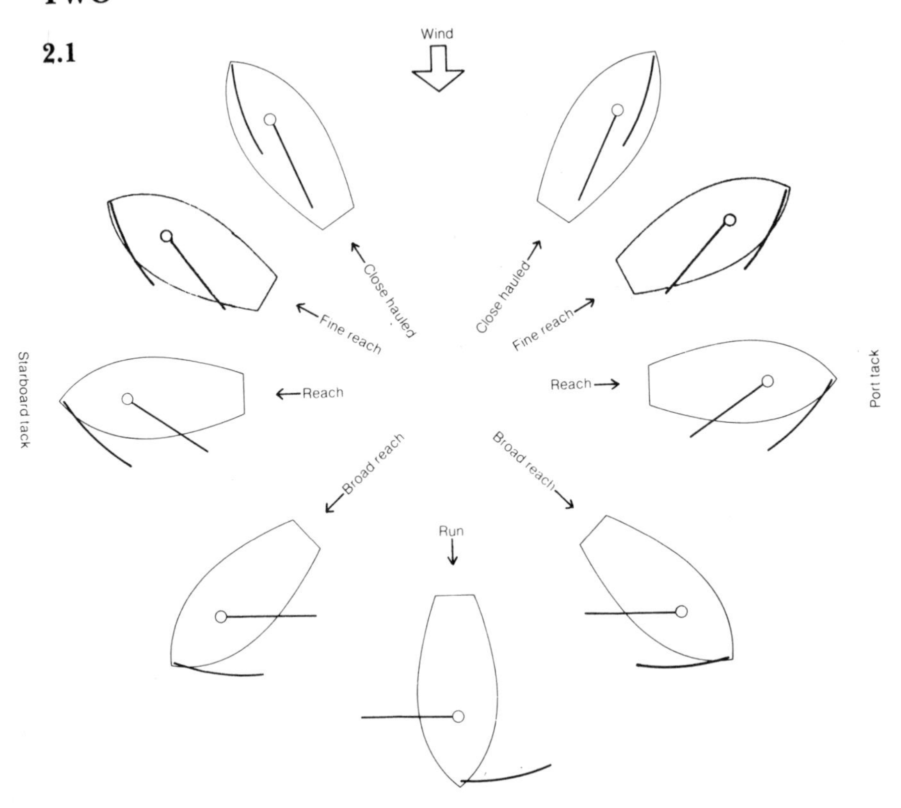

**2.2** I a. Bow line. b. Stern line. c. Breast lines. d. Springs.
II The bow and stern lines hold the boat's bows and stern in.
The breast lines keep the boat alongside.
The springs stop the boat moving fore and aft.
**2.3** a. Ring. b. Stock. c. Shank. d. Crown. e. Fluke.
**2.4**

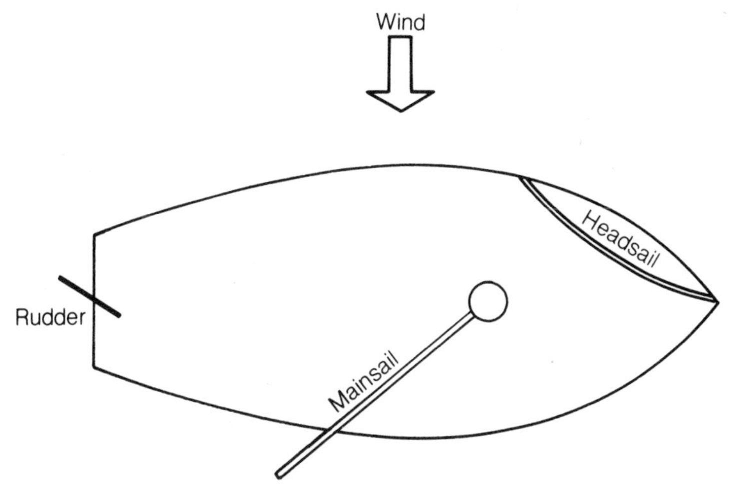


**2.5** A second anchor has been laid to stop the boat yawing.

## THREE

**3.1** a. Standing apart. b. Bight. c. End.
**3.2** I a. A stopper knot or figure of eight. b. A bowline.
c. A round turn and two half hitches.
II a. To stop the end of a sheet pulling through a block.
b. To put a temporary eye in a rope.
c. For securing a mooring line to a ring.
**3.3** She would probably be running before the wind with a storm jib only.
**3.4** Deviation 8° E.
**3.5** Variation. If the hand bearing compass is held well away from magnetic influences there should be no deviation.

**FOUR**

**4.1**

**4.2** To starboard.
**4.3** By taking bearings of shore objects at regular intervals.
**4.4** She can use clearing bearings from the lighthouse and the church to stay in safe water away from the rocks.
**4.5** I Withies
II They mark the safe channel.

## FIVE

**5.1** By taking a compass bearing at regular intervals. If the bearing does not alter the boat is on a collision course.
**5.2** b (a should go astern of b)
**5.3** The power boat.
**5.4** To create a clear airway.
**5.5** MAYDAY MAYDAY MAYDAY
THIS IS YACHT MERMAIN YACHT MERMAIN YACHT MERMAIN
MAYDAY YACHT MERMAIN
MY POSITION IS TWO FOUR ZERO LANDS END FIVE MILES
I AM SINKING AND REQUIRE IMMEDIATE ASSISTANCE
I HAVE SIX PERSONS ON BOARD
OVER

*Appendix I*

# Safety List for a Small Boat

The amount and type of safety equipment carried depends upon the size and type of boat and its cruising area. There are recommended lists in RYA booklet *G9* for craft under 13.7 metres. Racing boats may be subject to special rules.

Any boat of 13.7 metres and over must conform to the standards laid down in the Merchant Shipping Rules; below this size safety equipment is not compulsory but is strongly recommended.

A general guide is given below:

1. An approved liferaft of a size suitable to accommodate all persons on board, carried where it can be quickly launched.
2. A half inflated dinghy can be used instead of a liferaft but this is a poor alternative in anything but sheltered waters near the shore.
3. Two lifebuoys one with a light and a drogue and one with 30 metres of floating line (or a rescue quoit with floating line attached).
4. A dan buoy with a light and a drogue.
5. A lifejacket for every crew member.
6. A safety harness for every crew member.
7. Suitable safety harness anchorages.
8. Strong and adequate guardrails and lifelines.
9. An approved pack of flares with at least two red parachute rockets.
10. A first aid box.
11. A waterproof torch.
12. A method of securing and releasing the main hatch and hatch boards from either side.
13. The name of the boat on the spray dodgers and on a piece of canvas ready to display if necessary. Letters to be at least 22 cm in height.
14. A method of securing any heavy gear (such as batteries) so that

they will not damage the boat in heavy weather.

15. Adequate and efficient navigation lights.
16. Two anchors of sufficient size with enough warp and/or chain for the maximum expected depth.
17. One fixed and one portable bilge pump.
18. A radar reflector.
19. Sufficient up to date charts and pilot books.
20. A steering compass.
21. A hand-bearing compass.
22. A radio receiver for weather reports.
23. A radio direction finder.
24. A radio telephone (VHF).
25. A distance log.
26. A tow line.
27. A tool kit which includes a hacksaw and bolt cutters.
28. A separate engine battery which can be isolated from the lighting battery.
29. At least two fire extinguishers of an approved type.
30. A fire blanket.
31. A bag of sand for oil fires.
32. Two strong buckets with lanyards.

*Appendix II*

# Glossary

ABACK: A sail is aback when the wind strikes it on what would normally be its lee side.
ABAFT THE BEAM: The sector on both sides of a boat from abeam to astern.
ABEAM: The direction at right angles to the fore-and-aft line.
ABATE: The true wind abates or moderates when it blows less strongly than before.
ADRIFT: Not attached to the sea-bed.
AFLOAT: Floating; at sea.
AFT: Near or towards the stern.
AHEAD: The direction of an object beyond the stem of a boat.
AHOY: Shout to attract attention of another vessel.
ALEE: To leeward.
ALMANAC: An annual publication containing information on, for example, buoyage, tides, signals, glossaries, and positions of heavenly bodies.
ALOFT: Above deck.
AMIDSHIPS: The centre part of the boat.
ANCHOR BUOY: Buoy or float secured by a tripping line to the crown of the anchor.
ANCHOR CABLE: Chain or rope connection between a boat and her anchor.
ANCHOR LIGHT: An all round white light usually shackled to the forestay of a boat and hoisted to a suitable height by the jib halyard.
ANCHOR ROLLER: A roller over which the anchor cable is passed when at anchor.
ANCHOR WATCH: Watch kept when a boat is at anchor to check whether the anchor is dragging.
ANSWER THE HELM: A boat answers the helm when she alters course in response to the helmsman's deflection of the rudder.

APPARENT WIND: The wind felt by the crew in a boat that is moving over the ground.
ASHORE: On the land; or aground.
ASTERN: Direction beyond the stern; or a movement through the water in that direction.
ATHWARTSHIPS: At right angles to the centreline of the boat inside the boat.
AUTOPILOT: Equipment that allows the boat to follow automatically a compass course or a course relative to wind direction.
AUXILIARY: A term for a sailing boat that has auxiliary power, i.e. an engine.
AVAST: Order to stop an activity.
AWASH: Level with the surface of the water which just washes over an object.

BACK: To back a sail: it is sheeted or held to windward so that the wind strikes it on the side which is normally to leeward. Of wind: it backs when it shifts to blow from a direction that is further anti-clockwise.
BACK SPLICE: The end of a rope that has been finished by unlaying the strands, making a crown knot and tucking the strands back down the rope.
BACKSTAY: A stay which supports the mast from aft.
BACKWIND: Airflow that is deflected on to the lee side of a sail, such as a jib backwinding the mainsail.
BAIL: To remove water from the bilges or cockpit.
BALL: A black signal shape normally displayed by day when a boat is at anchor.
BALLAST: Additional weight placed low in the hull to improve stability.
BAR: A shoal close by a river mouth or harbour entrance; a measure of barometric pressure usually noted as 1000 millibars.
BARE POLES: No sails are set and the boat is driven by the force of the wind on the spars and rigging.
BARNACLE: A marine crustacean that attaches itself to the bottom of a boat.
BATTEN: A flexible strip of wood or plastic used to stiffen the leech of a mainsail.
BATTEN POCKET: A pocket on the leech of a mainsail to contain a batten.
BEACH: To run a boat ashore deliberately.
BEACON: A mark erected on land or on the bottom in shallow waters to guide or warn shipping.
BEAM: The breadth of a boat.

BEAM REACH: A point of sailing with the wind roughly at right angles to the fore-and-aft line.

BEAR: The direction of an object from an observer.

BEAR AWAY: To put the helm to windward so that the boat alters course to leeward away from the wind.

BEARING: The direction of an object from an observer given as an angle from a line of reference (true north or magnetic north).

BEARINGS (3 FIGURE NOTATION): Bearings and courses are given in a 3 figure notation, that is: 180° C or 180° T depending on whether it is a Compass or True bearing.

BEATING: Sailing towards an objective to windward following a zigzag course on alternate tacks.

BEAUFORT SCALE: A scale for measurement of the force of the wind.

BELAY: To make fast a line round a cleat or bollard.

BELL: In restricted visibility a bell is rung to indicate that a boat is at anchor or aground.

BELOW DECK: Beneath the deck.

BEND: To connect two ropes with a knot; to prepare a sail for hoisting; a type of knot.

BERTH: A place where a boat can lie for a period; a sleeping place on a boat; to give an obstruction a wide berth by keeping well clear.

BIGHT: A loop or curve in a rope or line.

BILGE: The rounded part of a boat where the bottom curves upwards towards the sides.

BILGES: The lowest part inside the hull below the cabin sole where bilge water collects.

BILGE KEEL: One of two keels fitted on either side of a boat's hull to resist rolling and provide lateral resistance.

BINNACLE: Strong housing to protect the steering compass.

BLANKET: To take the wind from another boat's sails.

BLAST (FOGHORN): A sound signal – a short blast lasts 1 second, a prolonged blast 4 to 6 seconds.

BLOCK: A pulley made of wood, metal or plastic.

BOAT-HOOK: A pole, generally of wood or light alloy, with a hook at one end, used for picking up moorings and buoys.

BOLLARD: Strong fitting, firmly bolted to the deck, to which mooring lines are made fast. Large bollards are on quays, piers and pontoons.

BOLT ROPE: Rope sewn to one or more edges of a sail either to reinforce the sides or so that the sail can be fed into a grooved spar.

BOOM: Spar that supports the foot of the sail.

BOOM OUT: On a run to thrust the genoa out to windward so that it fills with wind.

BOTTLESCREW: A rigging screw to tension the standing rigging or guardrails.
BOW: The forward part of a boat. A direction 45° either side of right ahead.
BOWLINE: A knot tied in the end of a line to make a loop that will neither slip nor jam.
BREAST ROPE: A mooring line that runs at right angles to the centreline; one runs from the bow and another from the stern to the shore or a boat alongside.
BROACH: With heavy following seas the boat can slew round uncontrollably, heeling dangerously.
BROAD REACH: The point of sailing between a beam reach and a run.
BROKEN OUT: The anchor, when pulled out of the seabed by heaving on the cable, is broken out.
BULKHEAD: A vertical partition below decks.
BUNK: A built-in sleeping place.
BUOY: A floating object used to indicate the position of a channel, wreck, danger, etc., or the position of an object on the seabed.
BUOYANCY AID: A life-preserver to help a person float if he falls in; less effective than a lifejacket.
BURGEE: A triangular flag worn at the masthead.

CABIN: The sheltered area in which the crew live and sleep.
CABLE: Chain or rope that is made fast to the anchor. A measure of distance equivalent to one tenth of a nautical mile.
CAPSIZE: The boat overturns.
CAST OFF: To let go a rope or line.
CENTREBOARD: A board lowered through a slot in the keel to reduce leeway by providing lateral resistance.
CHAFE: Damage or wear resulting from friction.
CHART: Printed map giving many details about the area covered by water and details about the adjacent land.
CHART DATUM: Reference level on charts and for use in tidal predictions.
CLEAR: To disentangle a line; to avoid a danger or obstruction; improved weather.
CLEAT: A fitting with two horns round which a rope is secured.
CLEVIS PIN: A locking pin with an eye at one end through which a split ring is fitted to prevent accidental withdrawal.
CLEW: The after lower corner of a sail to which the sheets are fitted.
CLEW OUTHAUL: The line which tensions the foot of the mainsail.
CLOSE HAULED: The point of sailing when the boat is as close to

the wind as she can lie with advantage in working to windward.

COACHROOF: The part of the cabin that is raised above the deck to provide height in the cabin.

COAMING: Vertical structure surrounding a hatch or cockpit to prevent water entering.

COAST RADIO STATION: A radio station for communication between ships at sea and the public telephone network.

COASTGUARD: The organisation responsible for search and rescue operations in UK waters.

COCKED HAT: In navigation the triangle formed when three position lines fail to meet at a single point.

COCKPIT: A space lower than deck level in which the crew can sit or stand.

COLLISION COURSE: The course of a boat which, if maintained relative to that of another, would result in a collision.

COMPASS ROSE: A circle printed on a chart representing the true compass and graduated clockwise from 0° to 360°.

CONE: A signal shape displayed either point upwards or point downwards.

COUNTER: Above the waterline where the stern extends beyond the rudder post forming a broad afterdeck abaft the cockpit.

COURSE: The direction in which the boat is being, or is to be, steered.

COURTESY ENSIGN: The national flag of the country being visited by a foreign boat; it should be flown from the starboard spreader.

CQR ANCHOR: A patented anchor with good holding power.

CRINGLE: A rope loop, usually with a metal thimble, worked in the edge of a sail.

DAN BUOY: A temporary mark to indicate a position, say, of a man overboard. A flag flies from a spar passing through a float and weighted at the bottom.

DECK LOG: A book in which all matters concerning navigation are entered or logged.

DEPTH SOUNDER: See Echo Sounder.

DEVIATION: The deflection of the needle of a magnetic compass caused by the proximity of ferrous metals, electrical circuits or electronic equipment.

DIAPHONE: A fog signal low pitched and powerful with a grunt at the end.

DIP THE ENSIGN: To lower the ensign briefly as a salute. It is not rehoisted until the vessel saluted has dipped and rehoisted hers in acknowledgement.

DIRECTION FINDER: A radio receiver with a directional aerial

with which the bearing of a radio beacon can be found.
DISPLACEMENT: The weight of a boat defined as the weight of water displaced by that boat.
DISTANCE MADE GOOD: The distance covered over the ground having made allowance for tidal stream and leeway.
DIVIDERS: Navigational instrument for measuring distances on charts.
DODGER: Screen fitted to give the crew protection from wind and spray.
DOUBLE UP: To put out extra mooring lines when a storm is expected.
DOUSE: To lower a sail or extinguish a light quickly.
DOWNHAUL: A rope or line with which an object such as a spar or sail is pulled down.
DOWNWIND: Direction to leeward.
DRAG: The anchor drags when it fails to hold and slides over the seabed.
DRAUGHT: The vertical distance from the lowest part of the keel to the waterline.
DREDGER: A vessel designed for dredging a channel.
DRESS SHIP: On special occasions ships in harbour or at anchor dress overall with International Code flags from the stem to the top of the mast and down to the stern.
DRIFT: To be carried by the tidal stream. The distance that a boat is carried by the tidal stream in a given time.
DRIFTER: A fishing vessel that lies to her nets.
DROP ASTERN: To fall astern of another boat.
DROP KEEL: A keel that can be drawn up into the hull.

EASE OUT: To let a rope out gradually.
EBB: The period when the tidal level is falling.
ECHO SOUNDER: An electronic depth-finding instrument.
ENSIGN: The national flag worn at or near the stern of a boat to indicate her nationality.
EPIRB: An Emergency Position Indicating Radio Beacon that transmits a distinctive signal on a distress frequency.
EVEN KEEL: A boat floating so that her mast is more or less vertically upright.
EYE: A loop or eye splice. The eyes of a boat: right forward.
EYELET: A small hole in a sail with a metal grommet through which lacing is passed.
EYE SPLICE: A permanent eye spliced in the end of a rope or wire rope.

FAIR: Advantageous or favourable, as of wind or tide.
FAIRLEAD: The lead through which a working line is passed in order to alter the direction of pull.
FAIRWAY: The main channel in a body of water such as an estuary or river.
FENDER: Any device hung outboard to absorb the shock when coming alongside and to protect the hull when moored alongside.
FETCH: The distance travelled by the wind when crossing open water: the height of the waves is proportional to the fetch and strength of the wind.
FIN KEEL: A short keel bolted to the hull.
FIX: The position of a boat as plotted on the chart from position lines obtained by compass bearings, direction finder, echo sounder, etc.
FLAKE DOWN: Rope laid down on deck in a figure of eight pattern so that it will run out easily.
FLASHING: A light used as an aid to navigation that flashes repeatedly at regular intervals.
FLOOD: The period when the tidal level is rising.
FLUKE: The shovel-shaped part of an anchor that digs into the ground.
FLYING OUT: A sail is flying out in a breeze when it has no tension in the sheets.
FOCSLE: The part of the accommodation below the foredeck and forward of the mast.
FOG: Visibility reduced to less than one thousand metres (approximately 0.5 nautical miles).
FOGHORN: A horn with which fog signals are made.
FOLLOWING SEA: Seas that are moving in the same direction as the boat is heading.
FOOT: The lower edge of a sail.
FORE-AND-AFT: Parallel to the line between the stem and the stern.
FOREDECK: The part of the deck that is forward of the mast and coachroof.
FOREHATCH: A hatch forward, usually in the foredeck.
FORESAIL: The headsail set on the forestay.
FORESTAY: The stay from high on the mast to the stemhead providing fore-and-aft support for the mast.
FOUL: The opposite of clear; adverse (wind or tide); unsuitable.
FOUL ANCHOR: An anchor whose flukes are caught on an obstruction on the seabed or tangled with the cable.
FRAP: Tie halyards to keep them off the mast to stop them rattling noisily in the wind when in harbour.

FREEBOARD: The vertical distance between the waterline and the top of the deck.
FREE WIND: The wind when it blows from a direction abaft the beam.
FRONT (AIR MASS): Boundary between air masses at different temperatures.
FULL AND BY: Close-hauled with all sails full and drawing; not pinching.
FULL RUDDER: The maximum angle to which the rudder can be turned.
FURLING: Rolling up or gathering and lashing a lowered sail using sail ties or shock-cord to prevent it from blowing about.

GALE: In the Beaufort scale, wind force 8, 34 to 40 knots. Severe gale, force 9, is 41 to 47 knots.
GELCOAT: The outer unreinforced layer of resin in a Glass Reinforced Plastic (GRP) hull.
GENOA: A large overlapping headsail set in light to fresh winds.
GHOSTER: A light full headsail set in light breezes.
GIVE-WAY VESSEL: The vessel whose duty it is to keep clear of another; she should take early and substantial action to avoid a collision.
GO ABOUT: To change from one tack to another by luffing and turning the bows through the wind.
GONG: A fog signal sounded in conjunction with a bell in a vessel over 100m in length when at anchor or aground.
GOOSENECK: Fitting which attaches the boom to the mast.
GOOSEWING: To fly the headsail on the opposite side to the mainsail (using a spinnaker pole or whisker pole perhaps) when running.
GRAB RAIL: Rails fitted above and below decks to grab at when the boat heels.
GROUND: To run aground or touch the bottom either accidentally or deliberately.
GROUND TACKLE: A general term for the anchors, cables and all the gear required when anchoring.
GRP: Glass Reinforced Plastic.
GUARDRAIL: Safety line fitted round the boat to prevent the crew from falling overboard.
GUNWALE: The upper edge of the side of a boat.
GUY: A line attached to the end of a spar to keep it in position.
GYBE: To change from one tack to another by turning the stern through the wind.

HAIL: To shout loudly to crew in another boat.
HALF HITCH: A simple knot.

HALYARD: A line or rope with which a sail, spar or flag is hoisted up a mast.

HAND-BEARING COMPASS: Portable magnetic compass with which visual bearings are taken.

HANDRAIL: A wooden or metal rail on the coachroof or below deck which can be grasped to steady a person.

HANKS: Fittings made of metal or nylon by which the luff of a staysail is held to a stay.

HARD AND FAST: Said of a boat that has run aground and is unable to get off immediately.

HARDEN IN: To haul in the sheets to bring the sail closer to the centreline; the opposite of ease out.

HATCH: An opening in the deck that allows access to the accommodation.

HAUL IN: To pull in.

HAWSE PIPE: A hole in the bow of a vessel through which the anchor cable passes.

HAZE: Visibility reduced to between 1,000 and 2,000 metres (0.5 to 1 nautical miles) by dry particles in suspension in the air.

HEAD: The bow or forward part of the boat. The upper corner of a triangular sail.

HEAD LINE: The mooring line or rope leading forward from the bows.

HEAD TO WIND: To point the stem of the boat into the wind.

HEADING: The direction in which the boat's head is pointing, her course.

HEADLAND: A fairly high and steep part of the land that projects into the sea.

HEADS: The lavatory on a boat.

HEADSAIL: Any sail set forward of the mast or of the foremast if there is more than one mast.

HEADWAY: Movement through the water stem first.

HEAT SEAL: To fuse the ends of the strands of a man-made fibre rope by heating.

HEAVING LINE: A light line coiled ready for throwing; sometimes the end is weighted.

HEAVING-TO: A boat heaves-to when she goes about leaving the headsail sheeted on the original side so it is backed. Ideal manoeuvre for reefing in heavy weather.

HEEL: To lean over to one side.

HEIGHT OF TIDE: The vertical distance at any instant between sea level and chart datum.

HELMSMAN: The member of the crew who steers the boat.

HITCH: A type of a knot.

HOIST: To raise an object vertically with a halyard.

HOLDING GROUND: The composition of the sea-bed that determines whether the anchor will hold well or not.
HULL: The body of a boat excluding masts, rigging and rudder.
HULL DOWN: Said of a distant vessel when only the mast, sails and/or superstructure is visible above the horizon.
HURRICANE: In the Beaufort scale, wind of force 12, 64 knots or above.
HYDROFOIL: A boat with hydrofoils to lift the wetted surface of her hull clear of the water at speed.
HYDROGRAPHY: The science of surveying the waters of the earth and adjacent land areas and publishing the results in charts, pilots, etc.

IALA: The International Association of Lighthouse Authorities which is responsible for the international buoyage system.
IMPELLER: Screw-like device which is rotated by water flowing past: used for measuring boat speed and distance travelled through the water.
IN IRONS: Said of a boat that stops head to wind when going about.
INFLATABLE DINGHY: A dinghy made of synthetic rubber filled with air; can be deflated for stowage on board.
INSHORE: Near to or towards or in the direction of the shore.
ISOBAR: On a synoptic chart, a line joining points of equal pressure.
ISOPHASE: A light where the duration of light and darkness are equal.

JAM CLEAT (SELF JAMMING): A cleat with one horn shorter than the other designed so that a rope can be secured with a single turn.
JIB: Triangular headsail set on a stay forward of the mast.
JURY RIG: A temporary but effective device that replaces lost or damaged gear.

KEDGE ANCHOR: A lightweight anchor used to move a boat or anchor temporarily in fine weather.
KEEL: The main longitudinal beam on a boat between the stem and the stern.
KETCH: A two-masted boat where the after (mizzen) mast is smaller and is stepped forward of the rudder stock.
kHz (KILOHERTZ): A measurement of frequency of radio waves equivalent to 1,000 cycles per second.

KICKING STRAP: Line or tackle to pull the boom down to keep it horizontal.

KINK: A sharp twist in a rope or wire rope; can be avoided by coiling the rope properly.

KNOT: The unit of speed at sea; one nautical mile per hour; a series of loops in rope or line.

LANDFALL: Land first sighted after a long voyage at sea.

LANYARD: A short length of line used to secure an object such as a knife.

LASH DOWN: To secure firmly with rope or line.

LAY: Strands twisted together to form a rope. To lay a mark is to sail direct to it without tacking.

LEAD LINE: A line marked with knots at regular intervals and attached to a heavy weight; used to determine the depth of water.

LEE: The direction towards which the wind blows.

LEEBOARD: A board or strip of canvas along the open side of a berth to prevent the occupant from falling out.

LEE HELM: The tendency of a boat to turn her bow to leeward.

LEECH: The trailing edge of a triangular sail.

LEE SHORE: A coastline towards which the onshore wind blows; the shore to leeward of a boat.

LEEWARD: Downwind, away from the wind, the direction towards which the wind blows.

LEEWARD BOAT: When two boats are on the same tack, the leeward boat is that which is to leeward of the other.

LEEWAY: The angular difference between the water track and the boat's heading. The effect of wind moving the boat bodily to leeward.

LIFELINE: A wire or line attached at either end to a strong point and rigged along the deck to provide a handhold or to clip on a safety harness.

LINE: Alternative name for small size rope or for a rope used for mooring a boat.

LINE OF SOUNDINGS: Numerous soundings taken at regular intervals.

LIST: A permanent lean to one side or the other.

LIST OF LIGHTS: Official publication giving details of lights exhibited as aids to navigation.

LIVELY: Said of a boat that responds rapidly to the seas.

LOA: Length overall.

LOAFER: A lightweight sail used when reaching or running in light winds.

LOCKER: An enclosed stowage anywhere on board.

LOCKING TURNS: A reversed turn on a cleat to make a rope

more secure; not advisable for halyards which may need to be cast off quickly.

LOG: A device to measure a boat's speed or distance travelled through the water. See Deck Log.

LOG READING: The reading of distance travelled through the water usually taken every hour from the log and recorded in the deck log.

LOOK-OUT: Visual watch; or the member of the crew responsible for keeping it.

LOOM: The glow from a light below the horizon usually seen as a reflection on the clouds.

LOP: Short choppy seas.

LOSE WAY: A boat loses way when she slows down and stops in the water.

LUBBER LINE: The marker in the compass which is aligned with the fore-and-aft line of the boat against which the course can be read off on the compass card.

LUFF: The leading edge of a fore-and-aft sail.

LULL: A temporary drop in wind speed.

MAINSAIL: The principal sail.

MAINSHEET TRAVELLER: The athwartships slider to which the mainsheet tackle is made fast.

MAKE FAST: To secure a line or rope to a cleat, mooring ring, bollard, etc.

MAKE HEAVY WEATHER: Said of a yacht which rolls and pitches heavily, making slow and uncomfortable progress.

MAKE SAIL: To hoist the sails and get under way.

MAKE WATER: To leak but not by shipping water over the side.

MARINA: Artificial boat harbour usually consisting of pontoons.

MARK: An object that marks a position.

MAROON: An explosive signal used to summon the crew when a lifeboat is called out.

MAST: The most important vertical spar without which no sail can be set.

MAST STEP: Fitting into which the mast heel fits.

MASTHEAD LIGHT: A white light exhibited near the masthead by a power-driven vessel under way.

MASTHEAD RIG: A boat with the forestay attached to the masthead.

MAYDAY: The internationally recognised radio telephone distress signal.

MEDICO: When included in an urgency call (Pan Pan) on the radio telephone, Medico indicates that medical advice is required.

MHWS (MEAN HIGH WATER SPRINGS): The average level of

all high water heights at spring tides throughout the year: used as the datum level for heights of features on the chart.

MIST: Visibility reduced to between 1,000 and 2,000 metres (0.5 to 1 nautical miles) due to the suspension of water particles in the air.

MIZZEN MAST: The smaller aftermast of a ketch or yawl.

MOLE: A breakwater made of stone or concrete.

MONOHULL: A boat with a single hull.

MOORING: The ground tackle attached to a mooring buoy.

MOORING RING: A ring on a mooring pile to which head and stern lines are secured.

MULTIHULL: A boat with more than one hull such as a catamaran or trimaran.

NAUTICAL ALMANAC: Official publication giving positions of heavenly bodies and other information to enable a boat's position to be established.

NAUTICAL MILE: Unit of distance at sea based on the length of one minute of latitude.

NAVEL PIPE: A pipe which passes through the deck to the anchor chain locker.

NAVIGATION LIGHTS: Lights exhibited by all vessels between sunset and sunrise.

NEAP TIDE: Tides where the range is least and the tidal streams run least strongly.

NEAR GALE: Wind of Beaufort force 7, 28 to 33 knots.

NOMINAL RANGE OF A LIGHT: Nominal range of a light is dependent on its intensity: it is the luminous range when the meteorological visibility is 10 nautical miles.

NOT UNDER COMMAND: A vessel unable to manoeuvre such as one whose rudder has been damaged.

NOTICES TO MARINERS: Official notices issued weekly or at other times detailing corrections to charts and hydrographic publications.

NULL: The bearing of a radio beacon at which the signal tends to disappear when the aerial of a direction finder is rotated.

OCCULTING LIGHT: A rhythmic light eclipsing at regular intervals so that the duration of light in each period is greater than the duration of darkness.

OFFING: The part of the sea that is visible from the shore. To keep an offing is to keep a safe distance from the shore.

OILSKINS: Waterproof clothing worn in foul weather.

ON THE BOW: A direction about 45° from right ahead on either side of the boat.

ON THE QUARTER: A direction about 45° from right astern on either side of the boat.
OPEN: When two leading marks are not in line they are said to be open.
OSMOSIS: Water absorption through tiny pinholes in a GRP hull causing deterioration of the moulding.
OUTHAUL: A line with which the mainsail clew is hauled out along the boom.
OVERCANVAS: A boat carrying too much sail for the weather conditions.
OVERFALLS: Turbulent water where there is a sudden change in depth or where two tidal streams meet.
OVERTAKING LIGHT: The white stern light; seen by an overtaking vessel when approaching from astern.

PAINTER: The line at the bow of a dinghy.
PAN PAN: The internationally recognised radio telephone urgency signal which has priority over all other calls except Mayday.
PARALLEL RULES: Navigational instrument used in conjunction with the compass rose on a chart to transfer bearings and courses to plot a boat's position.
PAY OFF: The boat's head pays off when it turns to leeward away from the wind.
PAY OUT: To let out a line or rope gradually.
PERIOD: Of a light, the time that it takes a rhythmic light to complete one sequence.
PILE: A stout timber or metal post driven vertically into a river or sea bed.
PILOT: An expert in local waters who assists vessels entering or leaving harbour. An official publication listing details of, for example, local coasts, dangers and harbours.
PILOT BERTH: A berth or bunk for use at sea.
PINCH: To sail too close to the wind so that the sails lose driving power.
PIPE COT: A spare berth on a pipe frame that hinges up when not in use.
PISTON HANKS: A hank on the luff of a staysail.
PITCH: The up and down motion of the bow and stern of a boat.
PITCHPOLE: A capsize in a following sea where the stern is lifted over the bow.
PLAY: To adjust a sheet continuously rather than cleating it. Movement of equipment such as the rudder in its mounting or housing.
PLOT: To find a boat's position by laying off bearings on a chart.

PLOUGH ANCHOR: An anchor shaped like a ploughshare similar to a CQR anchor.
POINT: The ability of a boat to sail close-hauled: the closer she sails the better she points. A division of 11° 15′ on the compass.
PONTOON: A watertight tank, usually between piles, that rises and falls with the tide.
POOPED: A condition of a boat in which a following sea has broken over the stern into the cockpit.
PORT HAND: A direction on the port or left hand side of a boat.
PORT SIDE: The left hand side of a boat when looking towards the bow.
POSITION LINE: A line drawn on a chart by the navigator.
POUND: A boat pounds in heavy seas when the bows drop heavily after being lifted by a wave.
PREVAILING WIND: The wind direction that occurs most frequently at a place over a certain period.
PREVENTER: A line rigged from the end of the boom to the bow in heavy weather to prevent an accidental gybe.
PRIVILEGED VESSEL: The stand-on vessel in a collision situation: she should maintain her course and speed.
PULL: To row.
PULPIT: Stainless steel frame at the bow encircling the forestay to which the guardrails are attached.
PUSHPIT: Colloquial term for the stern pulpit.

QUARTER: The side of the hull between amidships and astern.
QUARTER BERTH: A berth that extends under the deck between the cockpit and the hull.

RACE: A strong tidal stream.
RADAR REFLECTOR: An octahedral device hoisted or fitted up the mast to enhance the reflection of radar energy.
RADIO DIRECTION FINDER: A radio receiver with a directional aerial that enables the navigator to find the direction from which a radio signal arrives.
RAFT OF BOATS: Two or more boats tied up alongside each other.
RANGE OF TIDE: The difference between sea level at high water and sea level at the preceding or following low water.
RATE: The speed of a tidal stream or current given in knots and tenths of a knot.
RDF: Radio Direction Finder.
REACH: A boat is on a reach when she is neither close-hauled or running. It is her fastest point of sail.

READY ABOUT: The helmsman's shout that he intends to go about shortly.
RECIPROCAL COURSE: The course (or bearing) that differs by 180°.
REED: A weak high-pitched fog signal.
REED'S NAUTICAL ALMANAC: Annual publication containing information on positions of heavenly bodies, tides, tidal streams, harbour regulations, radio signals, etc.
REEF: To reduce the area of sail, particularly the mainsail.
REEF POINTS: Short light lines sewn into the sail parallel with the boom that are tied under the foot (or the boom itself) when the sail is reefed.
REEFING PENDANTS: A strong line with which the luff and leech are pulled down to the boom when a sail is reefed.
RELATIVE BEARING: The direction of an object relative to the fore-and-aft line of a boat measured in degrees from right ahead.
RELATIVE WIND: See Apparent Wind.
RESTRICTED VISIBILITY: Visibility restricted by rain, drizzle, fog, etc., during which vessels are required to proceed at a safe speed and to navigate with extreme caution.
RHUMB LINE: A line on the surface of the earth that cuts all meridians at the same angle. On a standard (mercator) chart the rhumb line appears as a straight line.
RIDE: To lie at anchor free to swing to the wind and tidal stream.
RIDGE: On a synoptic chart, a narrow area of relatively high pressure between two low pressure areas.
RIDING LIGHT: Alternative term for anchor light.
RIDING TURN: On a winch the situation where an earlier turn rides over a later turn and jams.
RIGGING: All ropes, lines, wires and gear used to support the masts and to control the spars and sails.
RIGHT OF WAY: Term used for the vessel which does not give way.
RISK OF COLLISION: A possibility that a collision may occur; usually established by taking a compass bearing of an approaching vessel.
ROADS: An anchorage where the holding ground is known to be good and there is some protection from the wind and sea.
ROLL: The periodic rotating movement of a boat that leans alternately to port and starboard.
ROLLER REEF: A method of reefing where the sail area is reduced by rolling part of the sail around the boom.
ROLLING HITCH: A knot used to attach a small line to a larger line or spar.
ROTATOR: A metal spinner with vanes which rotates when a boat

moves through the water actuating the log on board to which it is attached by a log line.
ROUND: To sail around a mark.
ROUND TURN: A complete turn of a rope or line around an object. The rope completely encircles the object.
ROUND UP: To head up into the wind.
RUBBING STRAKE: A projecting strake round the top of a hull to protect the hull when lying alongside.
RUDDER: A control surface in the water at or near the stern, used for altering course.
RUN: The point of sailing where a boat sails in the same direction as the wind is blowing with her sheets eased right out.
RUN DOWN: To collide with another boat.
RUNNER: A backstay that supports the mast from aft and can be slacked off.
RUNNING FIX: A navigational fix when only a single landmark is available. Two bearings are taken and plotted at different times making allowance for distance travelled.
RUNNING RIGGING: All rigging that moves and is not part of the standing rigging.

SACRIFICIAL ANODE: A zinc plate fastened to the hull to prevent corrosion of metal fittings on the hull.
SAIL LOCKER: Place where sails are stowed.
SAIL TIES: Light lines used to lash a lowered sail to the boom or guardrails to prevent it blowing about.
SAILING DIRECTIONS: Also called Pilots. Official publications covering specific areas containing navigational information concerning, for example, coasts, harbours and tides.
SAILING FREE: Not close-hauled; sailing with sheets eased out.
SALOON: The main cabin.
SALVAGE: The act of saving a vessel from danger at sea.
SAMSON POST: Strong fitting bolted firmly to the deck around which anchor cables, mooring lines or tow ropes are made fast.
SAR: Search and Rescue.
SCEND: Vertical movement of waves or swell against, for example, a harbour wall.
SCOPE: The ratio of the length of anchor cable let out to the depth of water.
SCUPPER: Drain hole in the toe-rail.
SEA ANCHOR: A device, such as a conical canvas bag open at both ends, streamed from bow or stern to hold a boat bow or stern on to the wind or sea.
SEA BREEZE: A daytime wind blowing across a coastline from the

sea caused by the rising air from the heating of the land by the sun.

SEA LEGS: The ability to keep one's feet in spite of the motion of the boat.

SEACOCK: A stop-cock next to the hull to prevent accidental entry of water.

SEAROOM: An area in which a vessel can navigate without difficulty or danger of hitting an obstruction.

SEAWAY: A stretch of water where there are waves.

SECURITE: An internationally recognised safety signal used on the radio telephone preceding an important navigational or meteorological warning.

SEIZE: To bind two ropes together.

SERVE: To cover and protect a splice on a rope by binding with small line or twine.

SET (SAILS): To hoist a sail.

SET (TIDAL STREAM): The direction to which a tidal stream or current flows.

SET SAIL: To start out on a voyage.

SHACKLE: A metal link for connecting ropes, wires or chains to sails, anchors, etc. To shackle on is to connect using a shackle.

SHAPE: A ball, cone or diamond shaped object, normally black, hoisted by day in a vessel to indicate a special state or occupation.

SHEAVE: A wheel over which a rope or wire runs.

SHEER OFF: To turn away from another vessel or object in the water.

SHEET: Rope or line fastened to the clew of a sail or the end of the boom supporting it. Named after the sail to which it is attached.

SHEET BEND: A knot used to join two ropes of different size together.

SHEET IN: To pull in on a sheet till it is taut and the sail drawing.

SHIPPING FORECAST: Weather forecast broadcast four times each day by the British Broadcasting Corporation for the benefit of those at sea.

SHIPPING LANE: A busy track across the sea or ocean.

SHIPSHAPE: Neat and efficient.

SHOAL: An area offshore where the water is so shallow that a ship might run aground. To shoal is to become shallow.

SHOCK CORD: Elastic rubber bands enclosed in a sheath of fibres, very useful for lashing.

SHORTEN IN: Decrease the amount of anchor cable let out.

SHORTEN SAIL: To reduce the amount of sail set either by reefing or changing to make a smaller sail.

SHROUDS: Parts of the standing rigging that support the mast laterally.

SIDELIGHT: The red and green lights exhibited either side of the bows by vessels under way and making way through the water.
SIREN: The fog signal made by vessels over 12 metres in length when under way.
SKEG: A false keel fitted near the stern which supports the leading edge of the rudder.
SKYLIGHT: A framework fitted on the deck of a boat with glazed windows to illuminate the cabin and provide ventilation.
SLAB REEF: A method of reefing a boomed sail where the sail is flaked down on top of the boom.
SLACK OFF: To ease or pay out a line.
SLACK WATER: In tidal waters, the period of time when the tidal stream is non-existent or negligible.
SLAM: The underpart of the forward part of the hull hitting the water when pitching in heavy seas.
SLIDE: A metal or plastic fitting on the luff or foot of a sail running in a track on the mast or boom.
SLIDING HATCH: A sliding hatch fitted over the entrance to the cabin.
SLIP: To let go quickly.
SLIPLINES: Mooring ropes or lines doubled back so that they can be let go easily from on board.
SLIPWAY: An inclined ramp leading into the sea.
SNAP HOOK: A hook that springs shut when released.
SNAP SHACKLE: A shackle that is held closed by a spring-loaded plunger.
SNARL UP: Lines or ropes that are twisted or entangled.
SNATCH: Jerk caused by too short an anchor cable in a seaway. To take a turn quickly around a cleat, bollard or samson post.
SNUG DOWN: To prepare for heavy weather by securing all loose gear.
SOLDIER'S WIND: A wind that enables a sailing boat to sail to her destination and return without beating.
SOLE: The floor of a cabin or cockpit.
SOS: International distress signal made by light, sound or radio.
SOUND: To measure the depth of water.
SOUNDING: The depth of water below chart datum.
SOU'WESTER: A waterproof oilskin hat with a broad rim.
SPAR: General term for all poles used on board such as mast, boom and yard.
SPEED MADE GOOD: The speed made good over the ground; that is, the boat speed corrected for tidal stream and leeway.
SPILL WIND: To ease the sheets so that the sail is only partly filled by the wind, the rest being spilt.
SPINDRIFT: Fine spray blown off wave crests by strong winds.

SPINNAKER: A large symmetrical balloon shaped sail used when running or reaching.
SPIT: A projecting shoal or strip of land connected to the shore.
SPLICE: A permanent joint made between two ropes.
SPLIT RING: A ring like a key ring that can be fed into an eye to prevent accidental withdrawal.
SPRAY HOOD: A folding canvas cover over the entrance to the cabin.
SPREADERS: Metal struts fitted either side of the mast to spread the shrouds out sideways.
SPRING TIDE: The tides at which the range is greatest: the height of high water is greater and that for low water is less than those for neap tides.
SPRINGS: Moorings lines fastened to prevent a boat moving forwards or backwards relative to the quay or other boats alongside.
SQUALL: A sudden increase of wind speed often associated with a line of low dark clouds representing an advancing cold front.
STANCHIONS: Metal posts supporting the guardrails.
STAND IN: To head towards land.
STAND OFF: To head away from the shore.
STANDING RIGGING: Wire rope or solid rods that support masts and fixed spars but do not control the sails.
STARBOARD SIDE: The right side when looking forward towards the bow.
STAYSAIL: A sail set on a stay.
STEADY: Order to the helmsman to keep the boat on her present course.
STEAMING LIGHT: Alternative term for masthead light.
STEERAGE WAY: A boat has steerage way when she is moving fast enough to answer to the helm; that is, to respond to deflections of the rudder.
STEERING COMPASS: The compass permanently mounted adjacent to the helmsman which he uses as a reference to keep the boat on a given course.
STEM: The forewardmost part of the hull.
STEMHEAD: The top of the stem.
STERN: The afterpart of the boat.
STERN GLAND: Packing around the propeller shaft where it passes through the hull.
STERN LIGHT: A white light exhibited from the stern.
STERN LINE: The mooring line going aft from the stern.
STERNSHEETS: The aftermost part of an open boat.
STIFF: A boat that does not heel easily; opposite to tender.
STOPPER KNOT: A knot made in the end of a rope to prevent it

running out through a block or fairlead.

STORM: Wind of Beaufort force 10, 48 to 55 knots; or a violent storm force 11, 56 to 63 knots.

STORM JIB: Small heavy jib set in strong winds.

STORMBOUND: Confined to a port or anchorage by heavy weather.

STOVE IN: A hull that has been broken inwards.

STOW: Put away in a proper place. Stowed for sea implies that all gear and loose equipment has, in addition, been lashed down.

STRAND: To run a vessel aground intentionally or accidentally.

STROP: A loop of wire rope fitted round a spar. A wire rope used to add length to the luff of a headsail.

STRUM BOX: A strainer fitted around the suction end of a bilge pump hose to prevent the pump being choked by debris.

STRUT: A small projecting rod.

SUIT: A complete set of sails.

SURGE: To ease a rope out round a winch or bollard.

SWASHWAY: A narrow channel between shoals.

SWEAT UP: To tauten a rope as much as possible.

SWEEP: A long oar.

SWING: To rotate sideways on a mooring in response to a change in direction of the tidal stream or wind.

SWINGING ROOM: The area encompassed by a swing that excludes any risk of collision or of grounding.

SYNOPSIS: A brief statement outlining the weather situation at a particular time.

SYNOPTIC CHART: A weather chart covering a large area on which is plotted information giving an overall view of the weather at a particular moment.

TACK: To go about from one course to another with the bow passing through the eye of the wind. A sailing boat is on a tack if she is neither gybing or tacking.

TACKLE: A combination of rope and blocks designed to increase the pulling or hoisting power of a line.

TAKE IN: Lower a sail.

TAKE THE HELM: Steer the boat.

TAKE WAY OFF: To reduce the speed of the boat.

TELLTALES: Lengths of wool or ribbon attached to the sails or shrouds to indicate the airflow or apparent direction of the wind.

TENDER: A boat that heels easily is said to be tender; the opposite of stiff.

THWART: The athwartships seat in a small boat or dinghy.

TIDAL STREAM: The horizontal movement of water caused by the tides.

TIDAL STREAM ATLAS: An official publication showing the direction and rate of the tidal streams for a particular area.

TIDE: The vertical rise and fall of the waters in the oceans in response to the gravitational forces of the sun and moon.

TIDE TABLES: Official annual publication which gives the times and heights of high and low water for standard ports and the differences for secondary ports.

TIDEWAY: The part of a channel where the tidal stream runs most strongly.

TILLER: A lever attached to the rudder head by which the helmsman deflects the rudder.

TIME (4 FIGURE NOTATION): Time is given in a four figure notation based on the 24-hour clock.

TOE-RAIL: A low strip of wood or light alloy that runs round the edge of a deck.

TOGGLE: A small piece of wood inserted in an eye to make a quick connection.

TOPPING LIFT: A line from the base of the mast passing around a sheave at the top thence to the end of the boom to take the weight of the boom when lowering the sail.

TOPSIDES: The part of a boat which lies above the waterline when she is not heeled.

TRACK: The path between two positions: ground track is that over the ground; water track is that through the water.

TRAFFIC SEPARATION SCHEME: In areas of heavy traffic, a system of one way lanes. Special regulations apply to shipping in these zones.

TRANSCEIVER: A radio transmitter and receiver.

TRANSDUCER: A component that converts electric signals into sound waves and vice versa.

TRANSFERRED POSITION LINE: A position line for one time, transferred, with due allowance for the vessel's ground track, to cross with another position line at a later time.

TRANSIT: Two fixed objects are in transit when they are in line.

TRANSOM: The flat transverse structure across the stern of a hull.

TRAVELLER: The sliding car on a track, for example on the main sheet track or adjustable headsail sheet block.

TRAWLER: A fishing vessel that fishes using nets trawled along the sea-bed.

TRICK: Spell on duty, espcially at the helm.

TRI-COLOUR LIGHT: A single light at the top of the mast of sailing boats under 20 metres long that can be used when sailing in place of the navigation lights.

TRIM: To adjust the sails by easing or hardening in the sheets to obtain maximum driving force.

TRIP-LINE: A line attached to the crown of an anchor to enable it to be pulled out backwards if it gets caught fast by an object on the sea-bed.
TROT: Mooring buoys laid in a line.
TRUCK: The very top of the mast.
TRYSAIL: A small heavy sail set in stormy weather on the mast in place of the mainsail.
TUNE: To improve the performance of a sailing boat or engine.
TWILIGHT: Period before sunrise and after sunset when it is not yet dark.
TWINE: Small line used for sewing and whipping.

UNBEND: To unshackle sheets and halyards and remove a sail ready to stow.
UNDERWAY: A vessel is underway if it is not at anchor, made fast to the shore or aground.
UNSHACKLE: To unfasten.
UNSHIP: To remove an object from its working position.
UP AND DOWN: Said of an anchor cable when it is vertical.
UPSTREAM: The direction from which a river flows.
UPWIND: The direction from which the wind is blowing.

VANG: A tackle or strap fitted between the boom and the toe-rail to keep the boom horizontal.
VARIATION: The angle between the true and the magnetic meridian for any geographical position.
VEER: Of a cable or line, to pay out gradually. Of the wind, to change direction clockwise.
VHF: Very High Frequency; usually taken as meaning the VHF radio telephone.
VISIBILITY: The greatest distance at which an object can be seen against its background.

WAKE: Disturbed water left by a moving boat. The direction of the wake compared with the fore-and-aft line of the boat is often used as a rough measure of leeway.
WARP: Heavy lines use for mooring, kedging or towing, and to move a boat by hauling on warps secured to a bollard or buoy.
WASH: The turbulent water left astern by a moving boat.
WASHBOARDS: Removable planks fitted in the cabin entrance to prevent water getting in.
WATCH: One of the periods into which 24 hours is divided on board.
WATERLINE: The line along the hull at the surface of the water in which she floats.

WEAR: To change tacks by gybing.

WEATHER A MARK: To succeed in passing to windward of a mark.

WEATHER HELM: The tendency of a boat to turn her bow to windward making it necessary to hold the tiller to the weather side.

WEEP: To leak slowly.

WEIGH ANCHOR: To raise the anchor.

WELL: A sump in the bilges. A small locker for the anchor.

WHEEL: The steering wheel that moves the rudder.

WHIPPING: Twine bound round the ends of a rope to keep it from fraying.

WHISKER POLE: Light spar to hold out the clew of a headsail when running, particularly when goosewinged.

WHISTLE: An appliance to make sound signals in restricted visibility and when manoeuvring.

WHITE HORSES: Breaking waves with foamy crest. Not surf breaking on the shore.

WINCH: A fitting designed to assist the crew hauling on a rope or line.

WINCH HANDLE: A removable handle used for operating a winch.

WINDAGE: All parts of a boat that contribute to total air drag.

WINDLASS: The winch used for weighing the anchor.

WINDWARD: The direction from which the wind blows.

WITHIES: Branches used in small rivers to mark the edges of the channel.

YANKEE JIB: A large jib set forward of the staysail in light winds.

YARD: A long spar on which a square sail is set.

YAWING: Swinging from side to side of the course set, or at anchor.

YAWL: A two-masted boat where the mizzen mast is aft of the rudder stock.

# Index